WHOSE STREETS? OUR STREETS!'

NEW YORK CITY: 1980-2000

CURATORS:

Meg Handler, Tamar W. Carroll, Michael Kamber, Josh Meltzer

INTRODUCTION BY:

Tamar W. Carroll

ESSAY BY:

Victoria W. Wolcott

WWW.WHOSESTREETS.PHOTO

Nina Berman
Bill Biggart
Donna Binder
Donna DeCesare
Maximo Colón
Ricky Flores
Frank Fournier
David Gonzalez
Lori Grinker
James Hamilton
Meg Handler
Lisa Kahane
Mike Kamber
Gabe Kirchheimer
Carolina Kroon
Corky Lee
Meryl Levin
Andrew Lichtenstein
Tracey Litt
Dona Ann McAdams
Thomas McGovern
Tomas Muscionico
Edwin Pagán
Brian Palmer
Clayton Patterson
Mark Peterson
Sandra-Lee Phipps
Sylvia Plachy
Alon Reininger
Richard Renaldi
Clarence Elie-Rivera
Joseph Rodriguez
Linda Rosier
Q. Sakamaki
Richard Sandler
Catherine Smith
Les Stone

Published by
Rochester Institute of Technology
1 Lomb Memorial Drive
Rochester, NY 14623

Distributed by

RIT PRESS

90 Lomb Memorial Dr.
Rochester, NY 14623
ritpress.rit.edu

ISBN-13: 978-0-692-13782-6

Library of Congress Control Number 2018950882

37 PHOTOGRAPHERS DOCUMENTED ORDINARY NEW YORKERS AS THEY RALLIED, MARCHED, AND DEMONSTRATED.

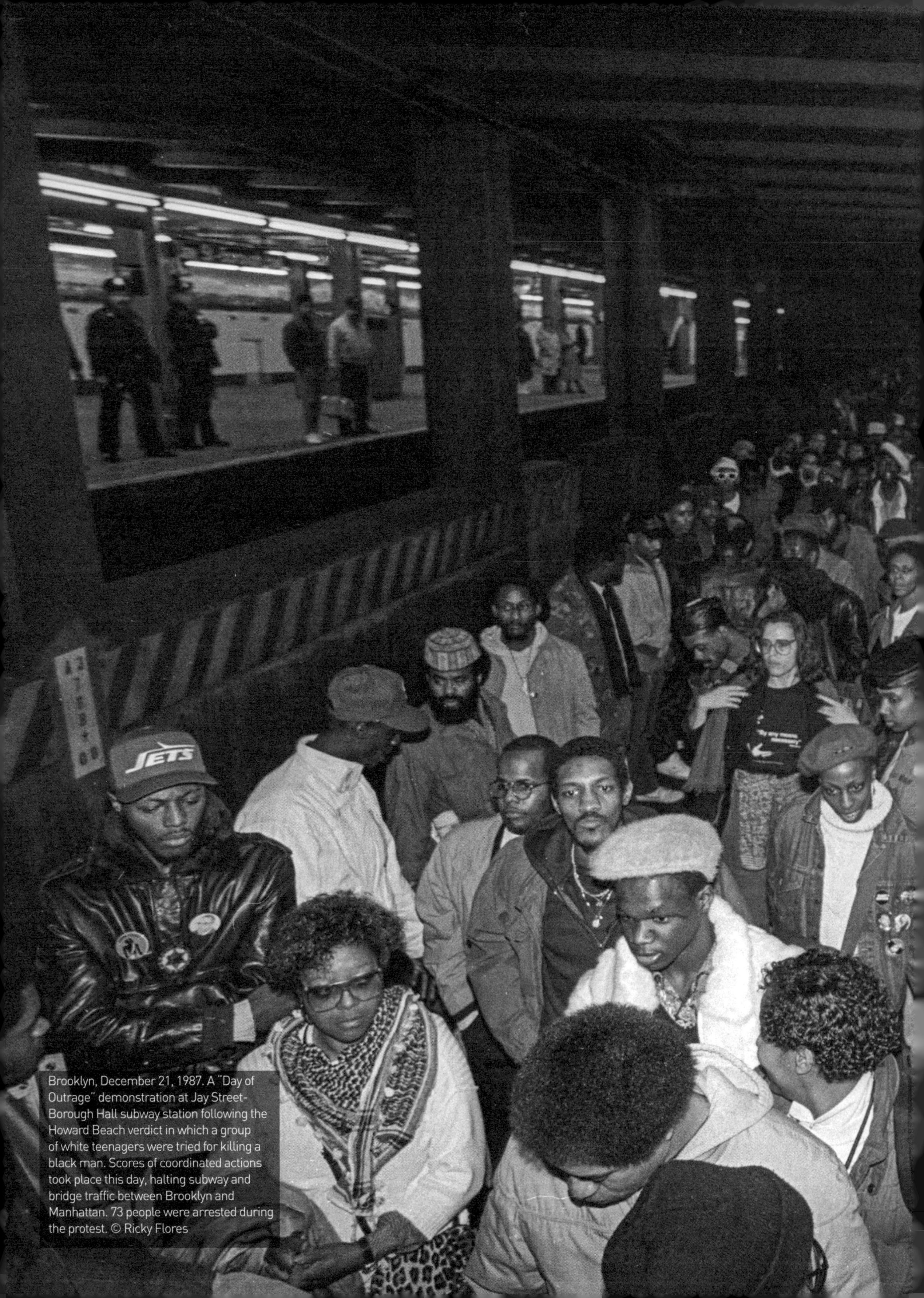

Brooklyn, December 21, 1987. A "Day of Outrage" demonstration at Jay Street-Borough Hall subway station following the Howard Beach verdict in which a group of white teenagers were tried for killing a black man. Scores of coordinated actions took place this day, halting subway and bridge traffic between Brooklyn and Manhattan. 73 people were arrested during the protest. © Ricky Flores

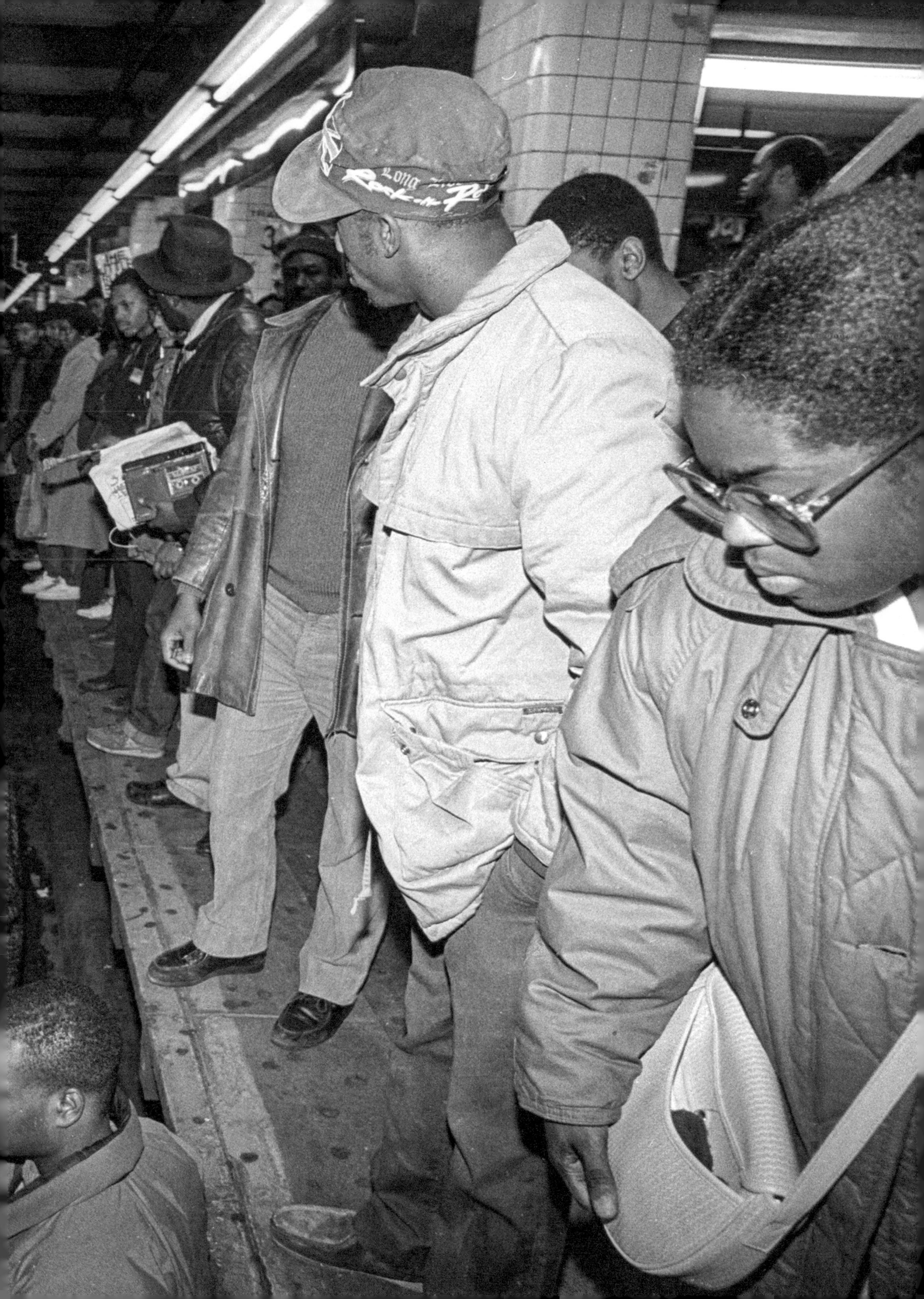

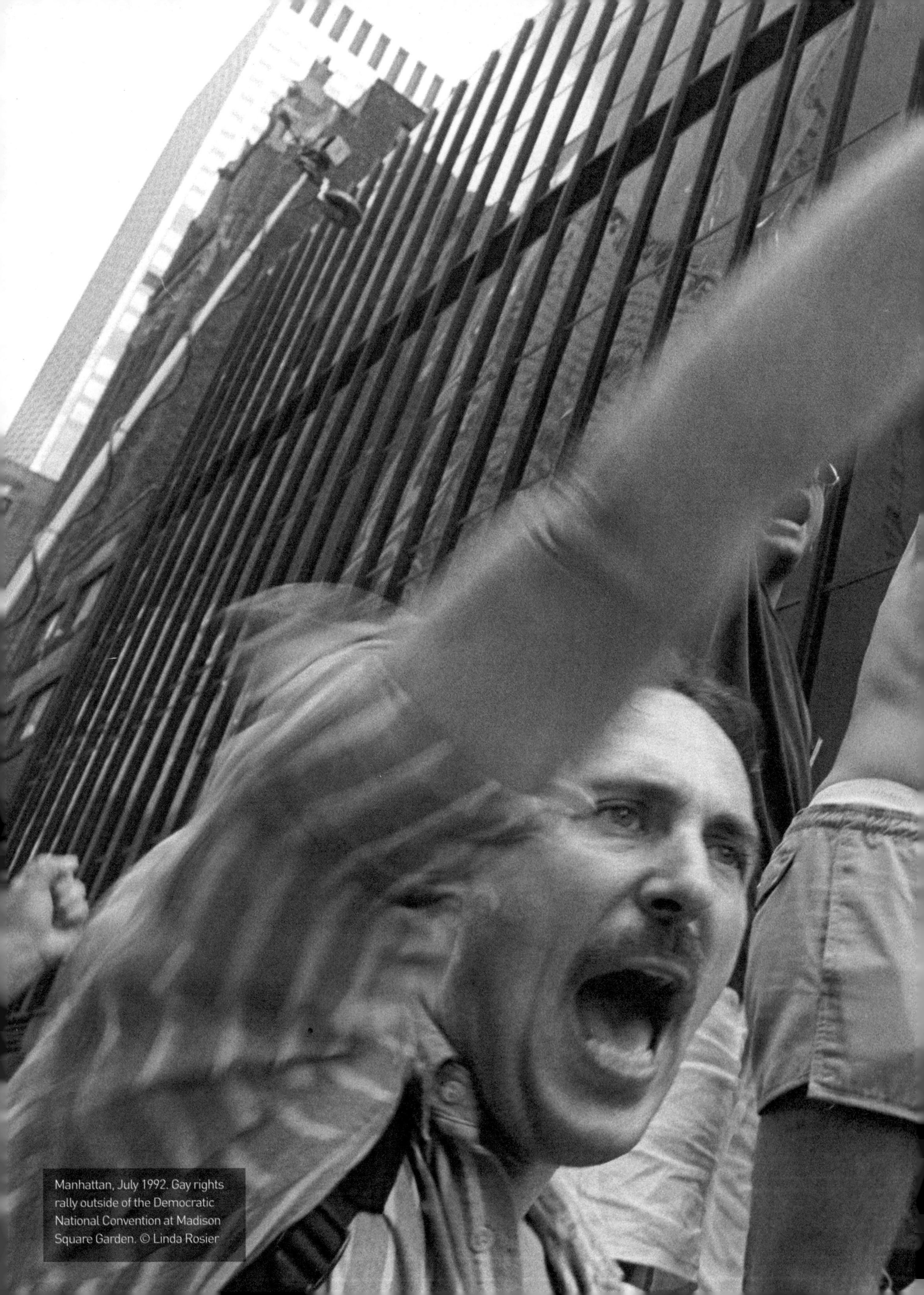

Manhattan, July 1992. Gay rights rally outside of the Democratic National Convention at Madison Square Garden.

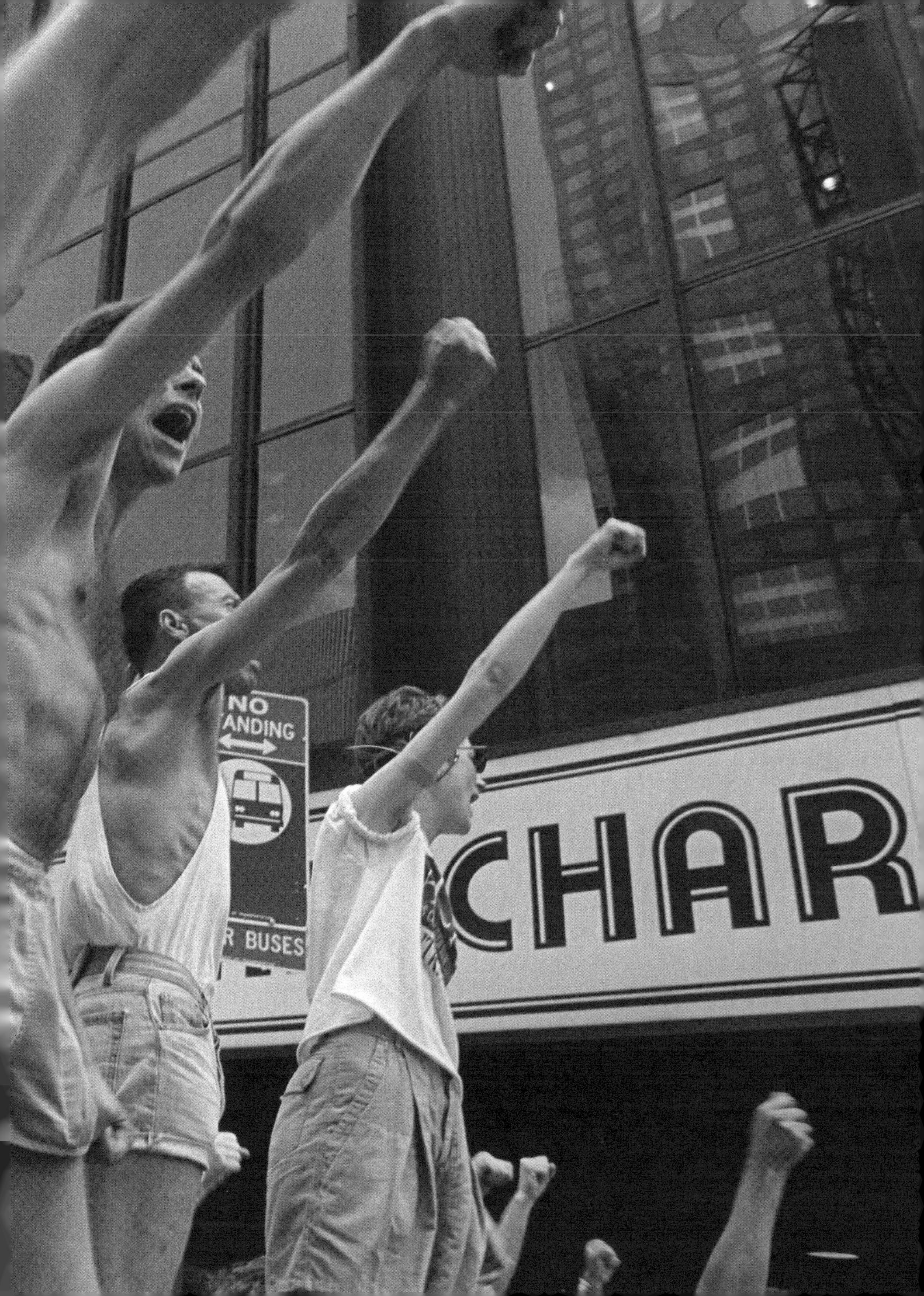
NO
ANDING
R BUSES
CHAR

'WHOSE STREETS? OUR STREETS!'

TAMAR W. CARROLL

NEW YORK CITY'S STREETS WERE TURBULENT IN THE 1980S AND 1990S, AS RESIDENTS RESPONDED TO SOCIAL CHANGES IN THEIR CITY AS WELL AS TO NATIONAL AND INTERNATIONAL DEVELOPMENTS.

The profoundly unequal economic recovery of the 1980s, dependent upon investment banking and high-end real estate development, led to heated contests over space and city services, as housing activists opposed gentrification and called attention to the plight of thousands of homeless New Yorkers. Immigration made New York City much more diverse, but a significant proportion of white New Yorkers opposed civil rights and acted to maintain racial segregation. Attempts to combat the high crime rates of the 1970s and early 1980s exacerbated concerns about police brutality, as innocent black and Latino New Yorkers died at the hands of the police. The culture wars wracking the nation resonated strongly in New York, a center of avant-garde art as well as of gay and lesbian and feminist activism, on the one hand, and home of the Vatican's spokesman in the U.S., Cardinal John O'Connor, and a significant culturally conservative Roman Catholic population on the other.

A cohort of photographers born between 1950 and 1970 committed themselves to documenting these struggles over social change as they unfolded, often in dialogue with each other. Progressive and independent, some published their work in The Village Voice, the nation's first alternative newsweekly, and some joined the cooperative photo agency Impact Visuals, dedicated to social documentary photography. Prior to the Bronx Documentary Center's exhibition in January-March 2017, the photographs presented here never had been displayed together. Collectively, they chronicle New York's history from 1980-2000. Work by each of the exhibition's 37 independent photojournalists is featured in this catalog, in alphabetical order by last names; additional photographs can be viewed on the companion website: www.whosestreets.photo.

The following essay provides historical context for the photographs and introduces the major themes of the exhibition. At a time in which elite control of the streets increased as did social and economic inequality, these photographs document ordinary New Yorkers' insistence on democratic participation in urban governance. In spite of the city government's efforts to contain disorder, residents used public spaces to demonstrate their views, taking disruptive actions together and forging collective identities in the process. Not all of these protests were progressive; white racial reactionaries and members of the Religious Right made their claims to privilege visible and public. Yet, on balance, the majority of activists documented here sought to further social justice and to expand understandings of citizenship. They claimed the streets, and thus the right to the city itself, for an expanded public, including visibly out LGBTQ people. Then, as now, documenting these moments and movements allowed photojournalists to expand their reach through time and space, amplifying their messages and helping activists reach new audiences.

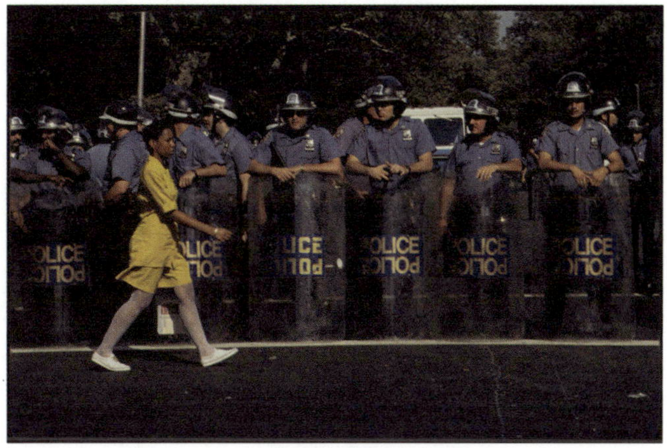

Brooklyn, 1991. A woman walks by a line of police during the Crown Heights riots in Brooklyn. © Mark Peterson

Race Relations

Racial tensions – linked to disputes about resource allocation, segregation, and crime and policing – dominated politics in New York City in the 1980s and 1990s. Residential segregation left poor neighborhoods like the South Bronx, with a majority African-American and Puerto Rican population, struggling to recover from the arson and abandonment of the 1970s, while real estate values in Manhattan soared. Democratic Mayor Ed Koch (1978-1989) alienated African-Americans and Latinos by closing Harlem's Sydenham Hospital in 1980, known for hiring African-American doctors and nurses when other hospitals' staff remained all white, and by failing to adequately respond to charges of police brutality and cases of racially motivated killings. In working-class white ethnic enclaves, some residents used violence to preserve racial segregation. Three black men--Willie Turks, Michael Griffith, and Yusef Hawkins--died at the hands of white mobs in the 1980s. In 1989 and 1990, civil rights leader the Rev. Al Sharpton staged protest marches through the largely Italian-American neighborhood of Bensonhurst to protest both Hawkins' killing and the acquittal of his accused assailant. White counter-demonstrators chanted racist slurs and held watermelons, a symbol of racist iconography dating back to the 19th century, and a 27-year-old, drunk white man stabbed Sharpton in the chest, nearly killing him.

Tensions boiled over in Crown Heights, Brooklyn, in August 1991, when an automobile accident in which two black children were struck, one fatally, by a Hasidic Jewish motorcade led to three days of rioting, including the killing of two white men by groups of young black men and anti-Semitic attacks on Jewish homes and businesses. The Crown Heights riots worsened race relations in general and particularly between blacks and Orthodox Jews, and contributed to Republican Rudolph "Rudy" Giuliani's 1993 mayoral victory over incumbent Democrat David Dinkins, the first African-American mayor of New York.

New Yorkers also eagerly read about and adopted strategies and tactics from national and international civil rights struggles; they were inspired by the South African anti-apartheid movement, the Puerto Rican nationalist movement, and the Asian-American civil rights movement.

Police Brutality

Excessive use of force, particularly against people of color, by the largely white police force was a major contributor to racial unrest in New York City in the 1980s and 1990s.

Among the most notorious cases were Michael Stewart, a 25-year-old African-American student who died in 1983 following a severe beating by NYC Transit Police arresting him for spray-painting graffiti in the subway; Eleanor Bumpurs, a 66-year-old mentally ill African-American woman killed in 1984 by police who came to evict her from her Bronx apartment; Jose (Kiko) Garcia, a 23-year-old Dominican immigrant killed in 1992 by police during a drug sweep (and whose death touched off rioting in Washington Heights); Anthony Baez, a 29-year-old Latino from the Bronx who died in 1994 after being choked during arrest (he had hit a police car with a football while playing catch with his brother); Abner Louima, a 30-year-old Haitian immigrant who was arrested and sodomized with a broomstick in a Brooklyn police station in 1997; Amadou Diallo, a 22-year-old Guinean immigrant fatally shot by police in the doorway of his Bronx apartment in 1999; and Patrick Dorismond, a 26-year-old African-American security guard killed in 2000 by undercover New York Police Department (NYPD) agents after they approached him to ask where they could purchase marijuana.

In some cases, activists also suffered from police brutality, including 27-year-old ACT UP member and former seminarian Christopher Hennelly, who suffered permanent brain damage after being clubbed on the head by police at an AIDS demonstration in 1991.

In 1993, in response to multiple high-profile cases of police brutality and despite vigorous opposition from police, Mayor Dinkins created the city's first Civilian Complaint Review Board. He was subsequently defeated in the mayoral election later that year by Giuliani, who pledged to crack down on crime. New Yorkers protested Giuliani's support for the NYPD despite the abuses in the Louima, Diallo, and Dorismond cases, as well as his support for Michael Meyer, an off-duty police officer who shot an unarmed "squeegee man" attempting to wash Meyer's car window. Many also opposed the Giuliani administration's adoption of the "stop and frisk" policy – later ruled unconstitutional – in which young African-American and Latino men were disproportionately targeted for searches by police.

Housing

During the fiscal crisis of the 1970s, during which New York City lost residents and manufacturing jobs and many landlords abandoned their buildings, widespread arson in low-income neighborhoods--including the South Bronx; East Harlem; and Bushwick, Brooklyn--led to a shortage of affordable housing. Rents also rose due to co-op conversion, which permitted landlords to convert vacant rental apartments into market-rate co-ops or condominiums. The result was record levels of homelessness by the 1980s, only recently surpassed by 2017's estimated 60,000 plus homeless residents.

Community groups such as the Committee to Save East Harlem opposed the displacement of long-term residents, often people of color, by gentrification while promoting the construction of affordable housing and the restoration of city services to low-income neighborhoods. AIDS activists drew attention to the plight of homeless People With AIDS (PWA), who were more likely to get opportunistic infections on the street.

The East Village was a particular flashpoint in conflicts over housing and homelessness in the 1980s and 1990s. The gentrification of buildings such as the Christodora House drew professionals and even celebrities to the neighborhood, historically home to waves of poor immigrants, including Puerto Ricans and African-Americans, who moved there in the 1950s and 1960s, along with members of the counterculture. Artists and housing activists had established "squats" in vacant buildings, restoring them and claiming ownership through sweat equity while citing landlords' failure to pay city taxes for more than 10 years. A large homeless tent encampment and an open-air drug market occupied much of Tompkins Square Park, to the consternation of city officials and some neighborhood residents.

In August 1988, police attempted to impose a 1 a.m. curfew on Tompkins Square Park and to clear it of homeless people; officers incited a riot by surrounding the park and violently charging the crowd, which included bystanders, neighborhood residents, homeless people, journalists, and housing activists. Over the objection of housing activists, the city closed the park from June 1991-July 1992, ostensibly for restoration but also to prevent homeless people from taking up residence. In May 1995, tensions flared again as police wearing riot gear and using an armored vehicle evicted squatters from two tenements on East. 13th Street.

Education and Labor

As manufacturing jobs continued their steep decline, the greatest areas of job growth in New York in the 1980s were in the highly paid financial services industry and in low-paying service-sector jobs, heightening income inequality and poverty. The recession of the early 1990s worsened conditions for many New Yorkers, who suffered from high unemployment rates well into the decade. Labor unions remained strong in New York, but were on the defensive, attempting to maintain workers' wages and benefits. In 1989, 60,000 telephone workers at NYNEX went out on a four-month strike, succeeding in resisting cuts to their medical benefits and changes in their wage structure in one of the most important anti-concession struggles of the era. In 1991, CUNY students walked out on strike, shutting down 6 of the 21 campuses and winning a reduction in a planned $52 million state budget cut and tuition hike.

New York added more than 800,000 immigrants in the 1980s and 1.2 million immigrants in the 1990s. By 2000, 45 percent of New York's adult population was foreign-born. This was a diverse group of migrants; in the 1990s, the largest groups came from the Caribbean (more than one-third), the former Soviet Union, China, Central and South America, Southeast Asia, Mexico, Poland, Korea, the Philippines, and Japan. Many recent immigrants worked as street vendors, domestic workers, and taxi drivers; in garment sweatshops and nonunion construction sites; or in the health care, restaurant, and retail industries. Labor activists worked to assist these workers and in some cases, to incorporate them into the union movement. In 1992, the ILGWU supported Mexican flower vendors' protests for the right to organize and to obtain licenses to legally sell flowers, preventing the police from seizing their highly perishable wares on the street. Worker centers, such as the Chinese Staff and Workers' Association, operated labor rights clinics to help workers redress wage theft and other labor law violations.

Health care workers fought against privatization of public hospitals and for living wages. In the 1990s, under the leadership of Dennis Rivera,

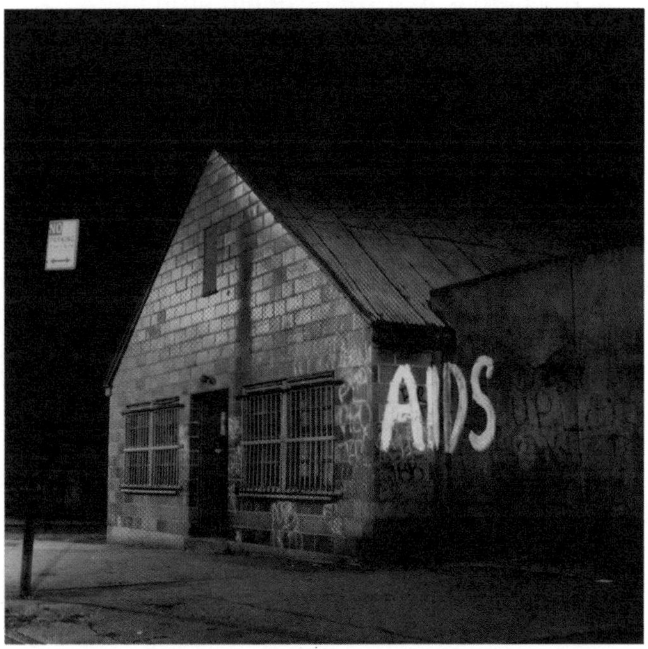

Brooklyn, 1987. Under the Williamsburg Bridge. © Sylvia Plachy

Local 1199, United Healthcare Workers East, which merged with the Service Employees International Union in 1998, grew by organizing nursing home and homecare workers in New York City and its suburbs, many of whom were immigrants.

AIDS

The early years of the HIV/AIDS epidemic were marked by uncertainty, false information, and fear about the cause and transmission of the disease. Despite having roughly half of the country's reported cases, New York City did not mount a systematic response to the emerging epidemic, and the care and housing of AIDS patients was left to volunteer groups such as the Gay Men's Health Crisis. Patients experienced stigma and neglect in the city's health care system. In 1985, parents in Queens launched a school boycott to protest the Board of Education's policy of allowing children with AIDS to attend public school.

The AIDS Coalition to Unleash Power (ACT UP), a direct-action group founded in 1987, used stunning visual art, spectacular street theater, and civil disobedience to draw attention to government inaction and the need for effective treatment and prevention to end the AIDS epidemic. ACT UP targeted prominent conservative Catholic leader Cardinal John O'Connor in its "Stop the Church" protests for his outspoken opposition to homosexuality, condom use, sex education in public schools, and abortion. AIDS activists also sought to draw attention to the archdiocese's role as a key provider of health and social services, including the city's first comprehensive-care ward for AIDS patients, which enforced religious directives barring discussion of condoms despite receiving substantial public funding.

AIDS activists succeeded in achieving many of their goals, including lowering the cost of and improving drug treatments for HIV/AIDS, involving patients in decision-making regarding medical research, and changing the definition of HIV/AIDS to incorporate opportunistic infections that affect women and poor people living with the virus. The extremely high death rates from the disease left many feeling desperate by the mid-1990s, however, and led ACT UP to stage political funerals, in which activists carried the bodies of people who died of AIDS through the streets of Manhattan.

Abortion Rights

In 1970, three years before the Supreme Court Roe v. Wade decision, New York State legalized abortion. Support for reproductive rights has historically been strong in New York City, home to a vibrant feminist community and groups such as the Committee for Abortion Rights and Against Sterilization Abuse (CARASA), which helped start the Reproductive Rights National Network, as well as the headquarters of Planned Parenthood, The Center for Reproductive Rights, and the American Civil Liberties Union. However, the influential leadership of the Roman Catholic Church mounted sustained opposition to abortion rights since the 1960s, financing and organizing what became known as the right-to-life movement and ensuring that Catholic hospitals refuse to perform abortions.

Abortion rights were hotly contested in the 1980s and 1990s, as a newly invigorated anti-abortion movement used street theater, civil disobedience, and violence to close clinics, while pro-abortion rights activists demonstrated in support of women's access to abortion and escorted patients into clinics. In 1988, when Operation Rescue founder Randall Terry encouraged anti-abortion activists to blockade clinics by chaining themselves to entrances, Cardinal O'Connor supported the actions and urged nuns to direct all their attention to ending abortion.

The 1989 Supreme Court *Webster v. Reproductive Health Services* decision restricting abortion rights reinvigorated the reproductive rights movement in New York City, as thousands rallied in support of abortion rights at Union Square Park. Webster upheld a Mississippi law banning abortion counseling, referral, or practice from any institution

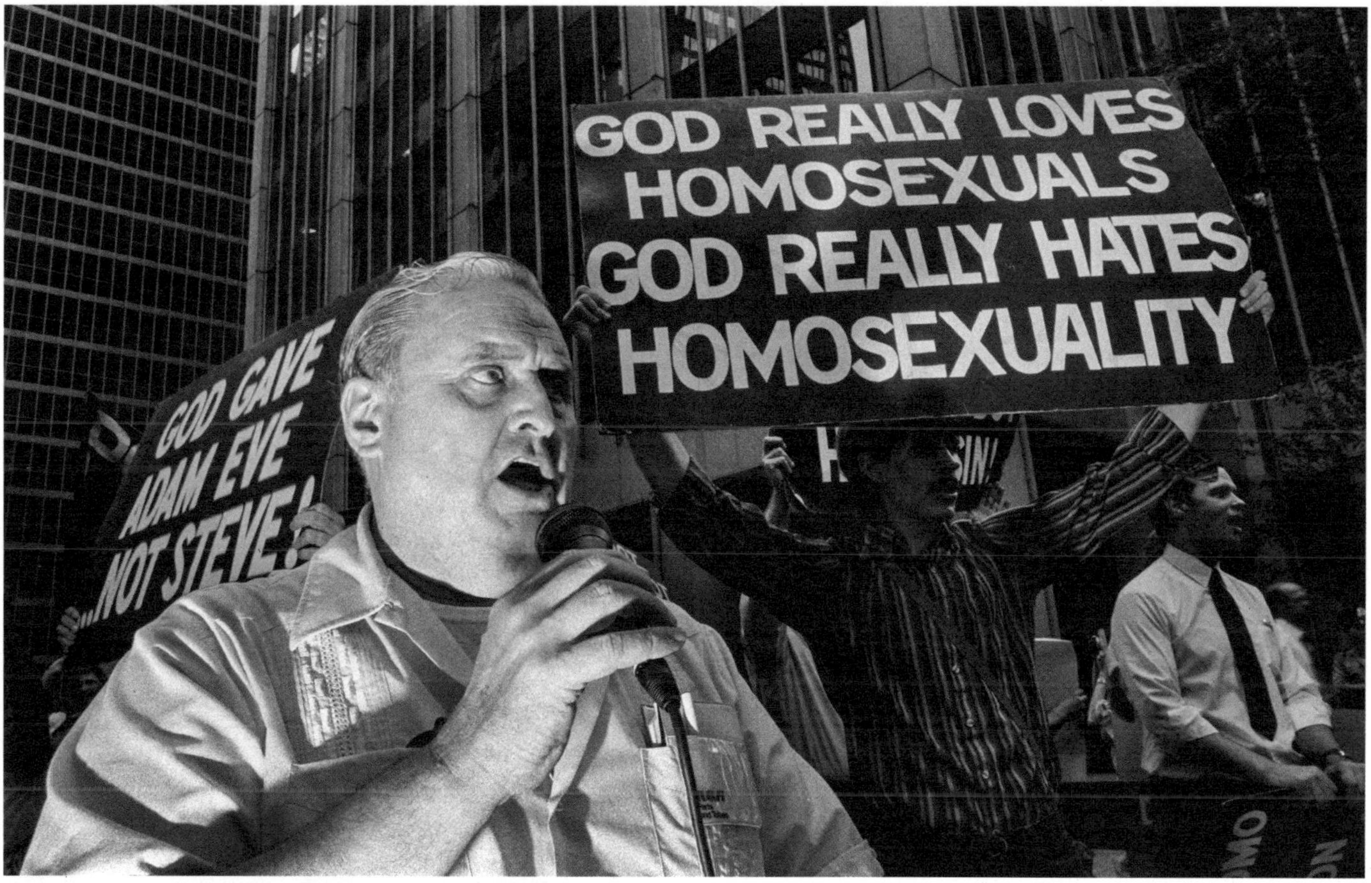

Manhattan, 1992. Anti-gay rights demonstration on 6th Avenue. © Richard Sandler

receiving public funding, unless it was to save a woman's life. The direction action group Women's Health Action and Mobilization (WHAM!) gagged the Statue of Liberty and joined forces with ACT UP in support of sexual freedom and the separation of sex and reproduction. Together, they attacked the Catholic hierarchy's antiabortion activities, opposition to birth control and sex education in public schools, homophobic rhetoric on AIDS, and opposition to homosexuality in the 1989 and 1990 "Stop the Church" protests, which drew thousands of participants.

The 1992 Democratic National Convention brought both pro- and anti-abortion rights activists to New York City, as both sides used striking visuals to gain coverage and get their messages out. Pro-abortion rights activists focused on women who died from illegal (or "coat hanger") abortions, while anti-abortion activists presented images of and actual fetuses, as Terry was arrested for arranging to have an allegedly aborted fetus delivered to Bill Clinton.

Culture Wars

The culture wars pitted the Religious Right against feminist and LGBTQ activists. This coalition of evangelical Protestants and Roman Catholics argued that the expression of sexuality outside of heterosexual marriage and the erosion of traditional gender roles were weakening the nation, and opposed abortion, homosexuality, and sex education in public schools. More broadly, the culture wars pitted traditionalists against progressives in areas including secularization, environmentalism, and animal rights.

In the late 1980s, censorship of the arts became a hot issue in the culture wars, as conservative Christians attacked representations of gay and lesbian sexuality, which they argued were obscene and unfit for public viewing. In 1989, Senator Jesse Helms (R-NC) initiated a campaign against the National Endowment for the Arts (NEA) for its support of exhibitions featuring the work of artists Andres Serrano, whose "Piss Christ" was intended as a protest the commercialization of sacred imagery, and Robert Mapplethorpe, whose photographs included men having sex with men. Helms got Congress to pass a ban on funding for "obscene" art, which resulted in the NEA withdrawing funding from several New York City-based exhibits that focused on AIDS in 1989 and 1990.

In 1999, Giuliani threatened to withdraw city funding for and evict the Brooklyn Museum for its "Sensation" exhibit, which included The Holy Virgin Mary by Chris Ofili, a black Madonna decorated with resin-covered elephant dung and surrounded by cuts-outs from pornographic pictures, which Giuliani and Cardinal O'Connor claimed was an attack on Catholicism. A federal judge ordered the city to restore the Museum's funding and cease eviction proceedings.

Feminists responded to the Religious Right's backlash with counter-demonstrations, but also mounted their own campaigns. In the 1980s and 1990s, direct action feminist groups, including the Guerrilla Girls, so named for the masks they wore to remain anonymous; and Women's Action Coalition (WAC) staged theatrical demonstrations at New York museums and designed eye-catching graphic posters to call attention to the paucity of work by women and artists of color in major collections. Feminists picketed outside rape and sexual assault trials, calling for an end to sexual violence. In 1992, WAC staged a Mother's Day demonstration at Grand Central Station to draw attention to the feminization of poverty, as divorce and low wages for women left single mothers and their children the poorest groups of Americans.

Queer Activism

In the early 1990s, queer activists sought to broaden the gay and lesbian movement to incorporate bisexual and transgender people, and more fundamentally, to reject binary sexual and gender categories such as "straight" and "gay." New York City was a center of queer activism in the 1990s. AIDS activists formed Queer Nation in March 1990 in response to increased violence against LGBTQ people on the streets of New York. They marched in protests of attacks, and staged "kiss-ins" at straight bars and nightclubs to increase the visibility and affirm the sexuality of LGBTQ people. Members of Queer Nation formed Pink Panther Patrol, a neighborhood watch group that conducted street patrols in the East and West Villages to combat homophobic violence.

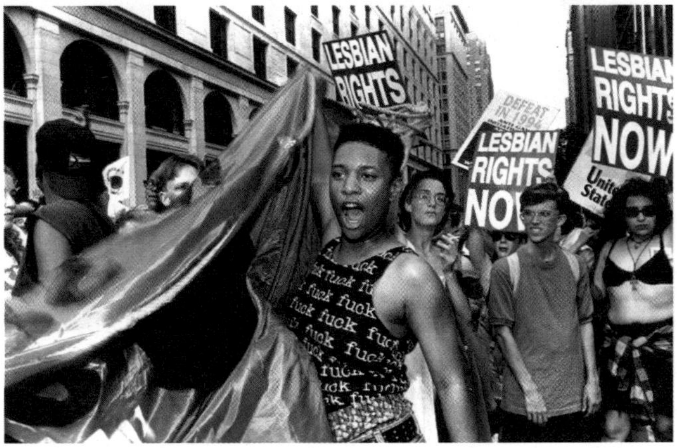

Manhattan, 1995. The Lesbian Avengers, a direct-action group dedicated to increasing lesbian visibility, organized the first Dyke March from 5th Avenue from Bryant to Washington Parks. The march became an annual event. ©Carolina Kroon

The Lesbian Avengers formed in New York in 1992 to promote lesbian visibility, in part through dramatic street theater, including fire eating, which the Avengers first practiced in response to the deaths of a lesbian and gay man who were burned to death after a Molotov cocktail was thrown into their apartment. To counter lesbian invisibility within the LGBTQ community, the Avengers organized the first Dyke March at the April 1993 March on Washington for Lesbian, Gay, and Bi Equal Rights and Liberation, with 20,000 women joining in. In June 1993, the Lesbian Avengers organized a New York City Dyke March the day before New York City's Pride March; the Dyke March since has become an annual event.

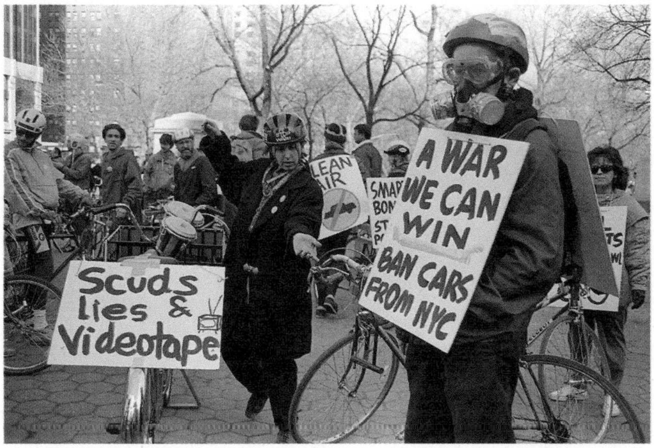

Manhattan, February 9, 1991. Cyclists prepare for a ride to protest the Gulf War and to promote bicycles as an alternative to car traffic in the city. © Lisa Kahane

War and Environment

As a city of immigrants and the home of the United Nations, New York has a long history of engagement with world affairs. In the early 1980s, one million people gathered in Central Park in support of the Nuclear Freeze Movement, urging the U.S. and the Soviet Union to stop the nuclear arms race and prevent the environmental disaster of a nuclear winter. The Central American Solidarity Movement sought to draw attention to the deaths of thousands of civilians at the hands of U.S. backed-militaries in Nicaragua, El Salvador, and Guatemala; to offer support to activists in those countries working to secure human rights; and to change U.S. foreign policy in Central America. New Yorkers marched and cycled in opposition to the 1990-91 U.S.-led Gulf War against Iraq; counterdemonstrators celebrated American nationalism and urged support for the military. Activists staged protests of religious conflicts in Ireland and the Middle East, appealing to ethnic communities within New York and drawing on the city's status as a global media hub to get their message out.

Environmental justice activists drew attention to high rates of pollution and asthma in low-income, minority-majority neighborhoods in New York City, as well as to the growth in the number of waste processing and power plants in these communities, a result of privatization and deregulation. In the 1980s and 1990s, activists opposed the construction or expansion of incinerators, waste treatment facilities, and power plants in Sunset Park, Williamsburg, Brooklyn, West Harlem, and the South Bronx.

Many activists drew connections between military and environmental policies as warfare caused environmental degradation, including the burning of oil wells in Kuwait and Iraq, and military spending put pressure on federal budgets, making funding for environmental protection more difficult to secure.

Conclusion

Collectively, the exhibition's photographs help us understand how today's New York came into being, including the battles for social justice that were won and lost and those that remain ongoing. More broadly, they provide a lens for thinking about recent history more broadly, as many of these social issues have shaped life in cities across the U.S. and the globe in recent decades. As 20th-century American historian Victoria Wolcott charts in her concluding essay to this volume, participants in these struggles are inextricably linked to those who participated in the social movements of the 1960s and to activists today, sharing the practices of participatory democracy and seeking to document for posterity their efforts to bring a better world to fruition. Thanks to the extraordinary work of the photojournalists featured in this catalog, we have much to learn from activists and documentarians alike.

Tamar W. Carroll is Associate Professor of History at Rochester Institute of Technology. She is author of the book Mobilizing New York: AIDS, Antipoverty, and Feminist Activism.

EXHIBITION

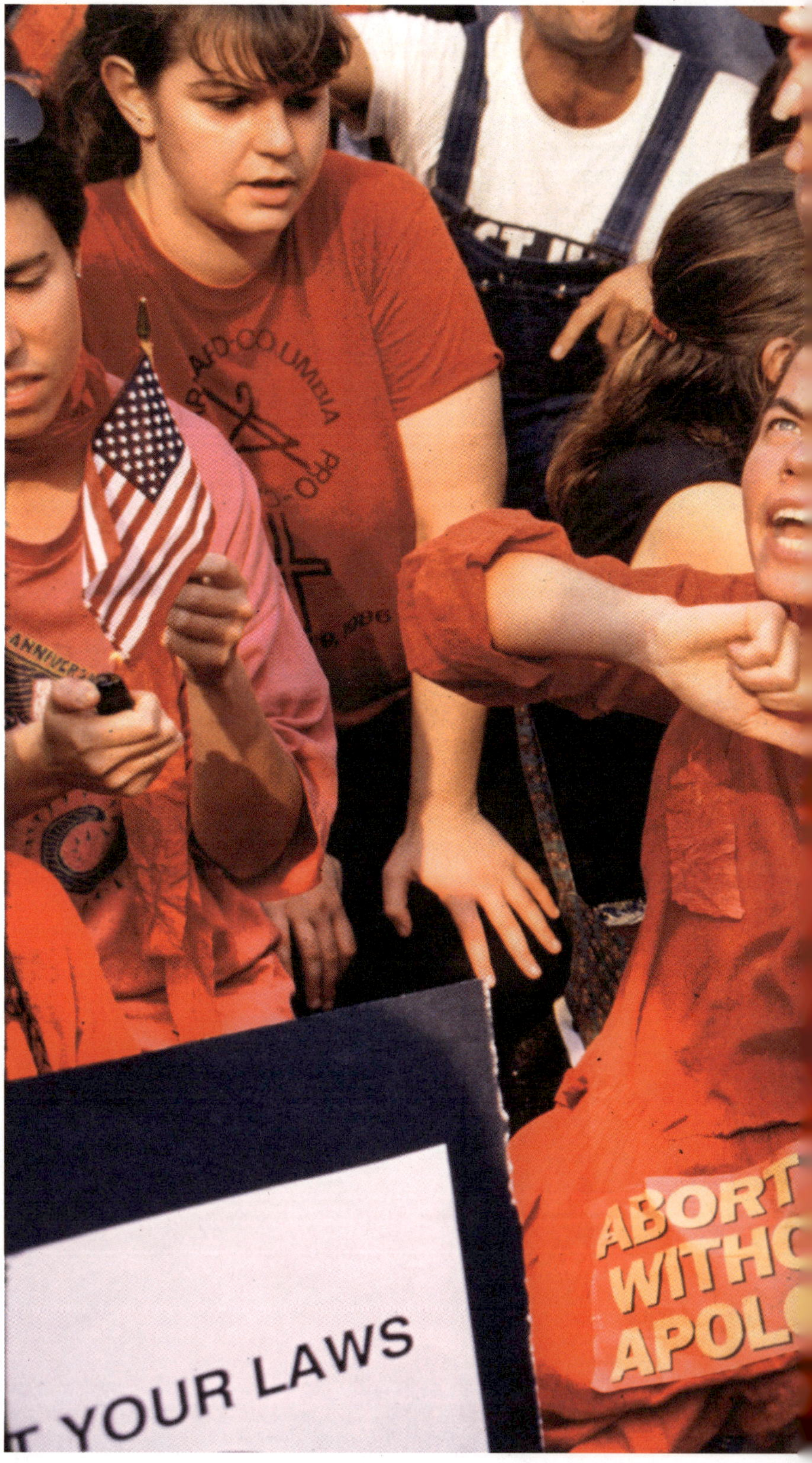

Manhattan, 1992. WAC (Women's Action Coalition) pro-choice protest during the Democratic National Convention.

NINA BERMAN

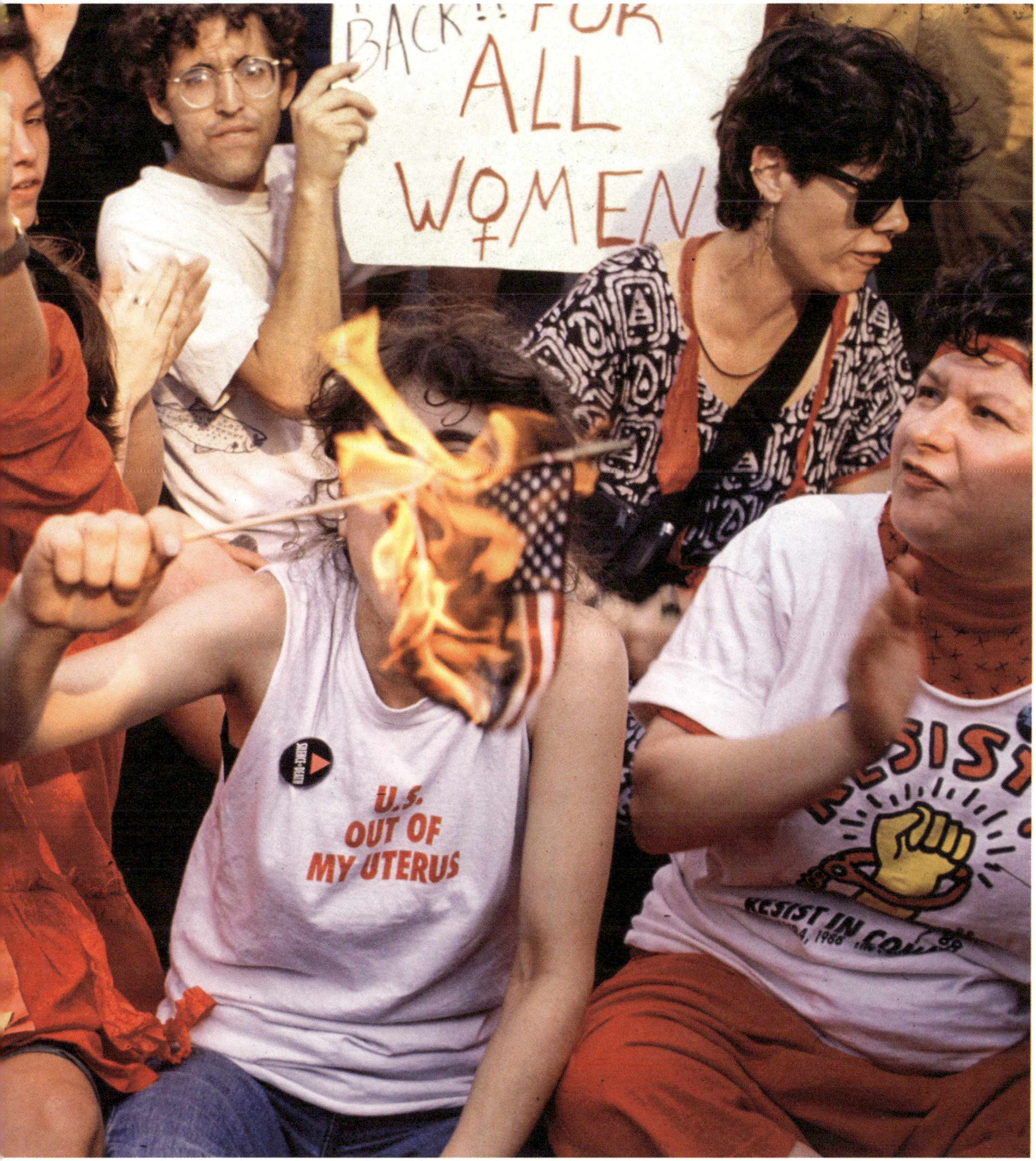

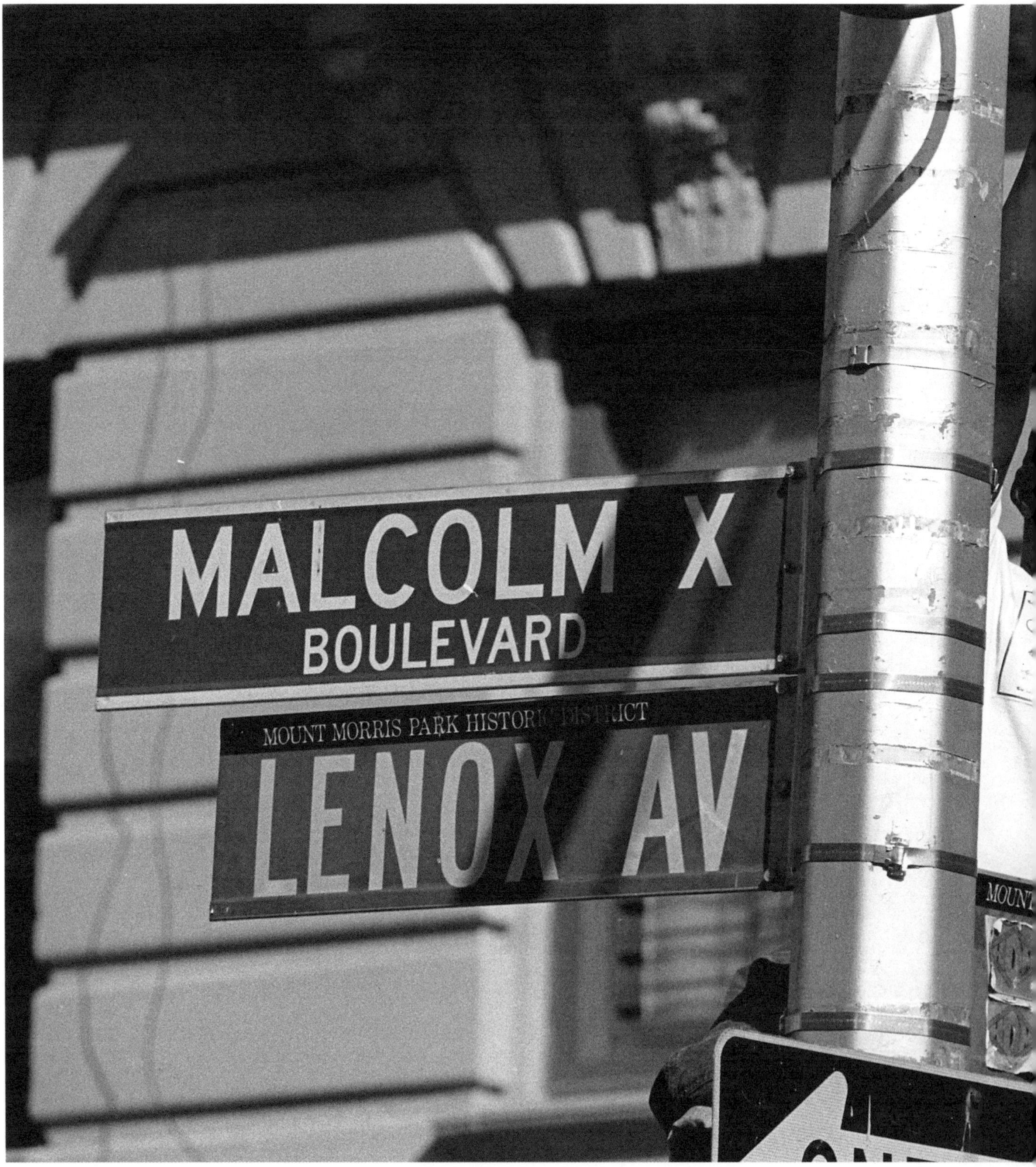
MALCOLM X
BOULEVARD
MOUNT MORRIS PARK HISTORIC DISTRICT
LENOX AV

BILL BIGGART

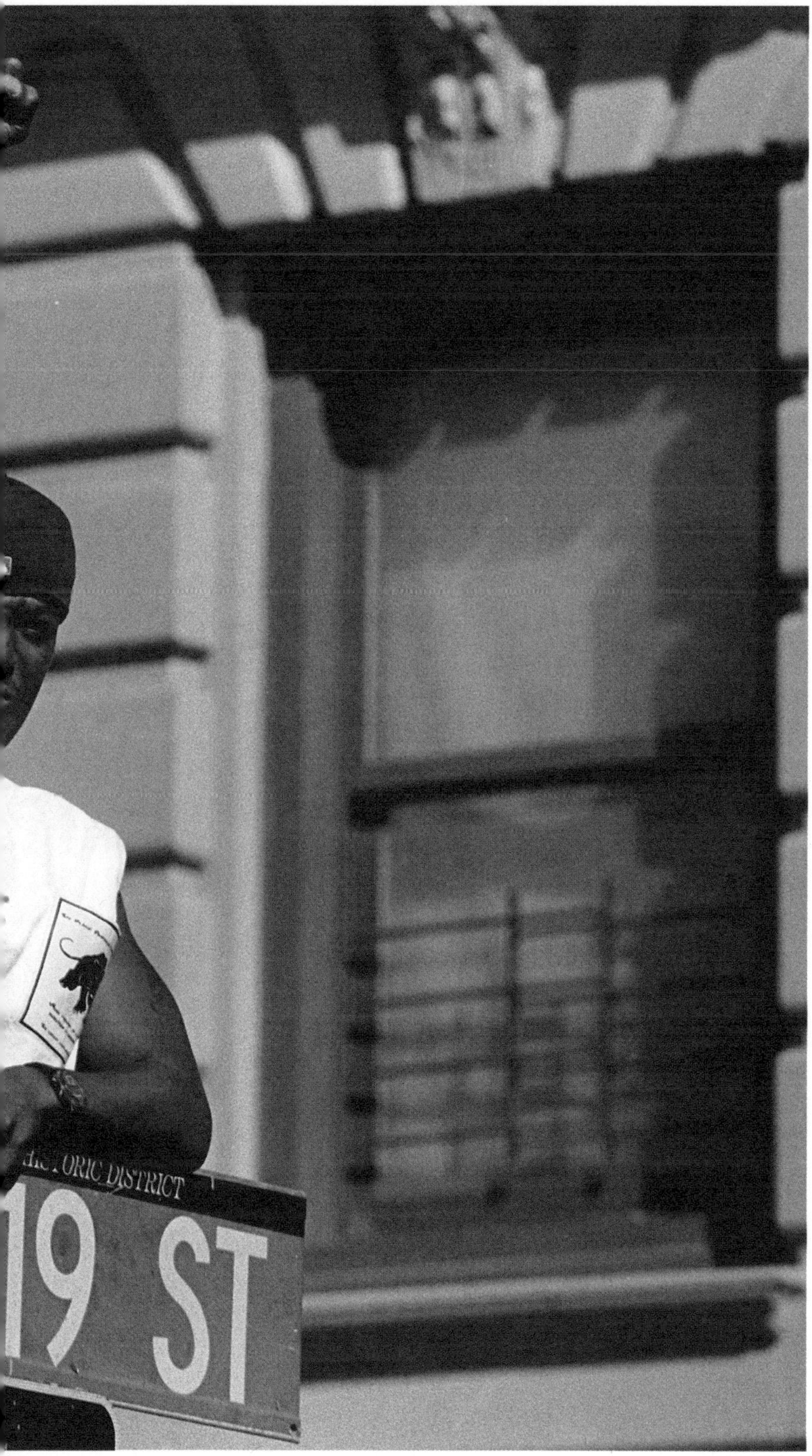

Manhattan, September 6, 1998. A protester at the Million Youth March in Harlem. The march was peaceful until the police ended the event by breaking up the crowds and making everyone leave.

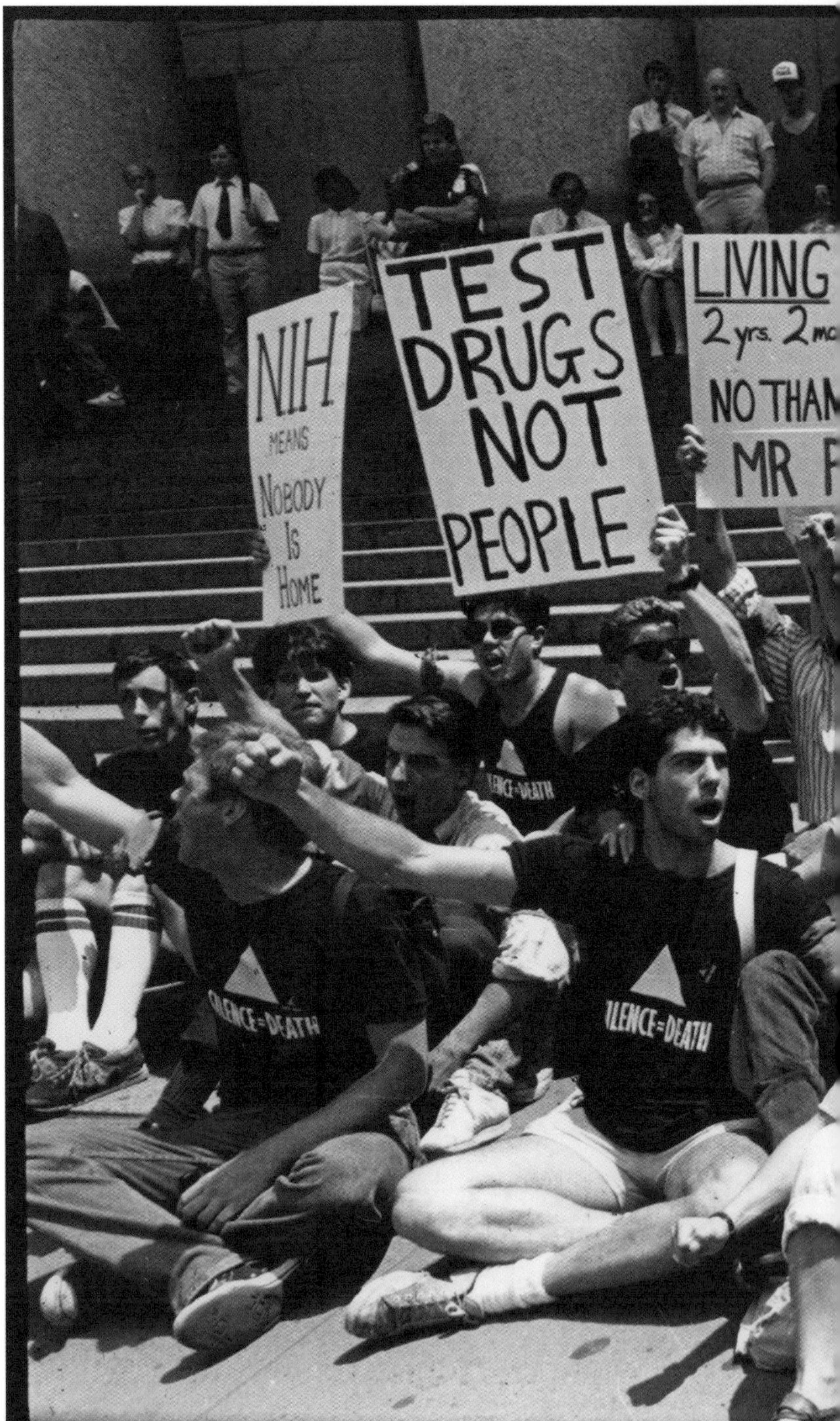

Manhattan, June 30, 1987. ACT UP members hold a demonstration and civil disobedience at Federal Plaza to protest President Reagan's inaction in the face of the AIDS epidemic, and to push for AIDS drugs, research and funding. The organization was founded in the same year.

DONNA BINDER

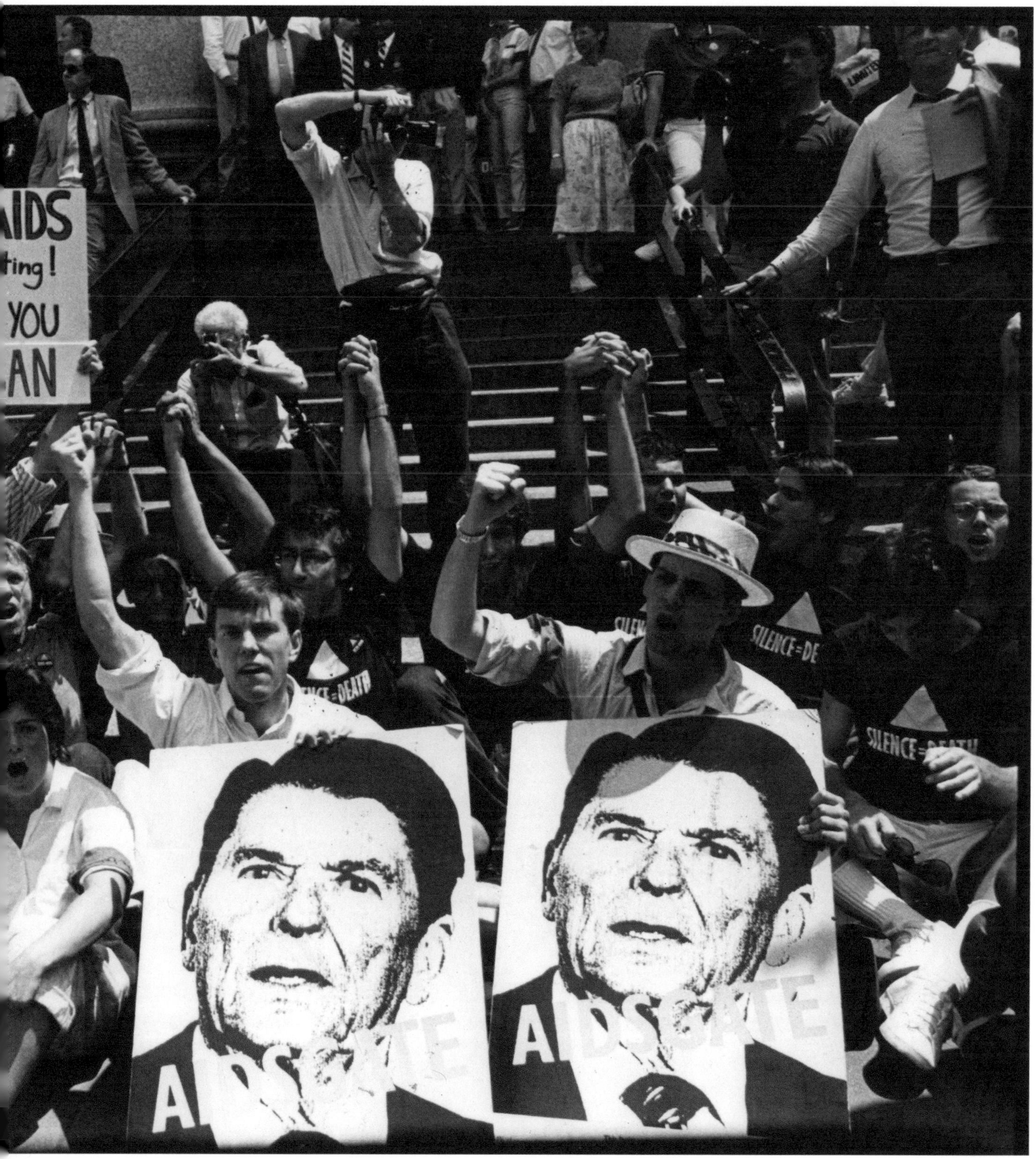

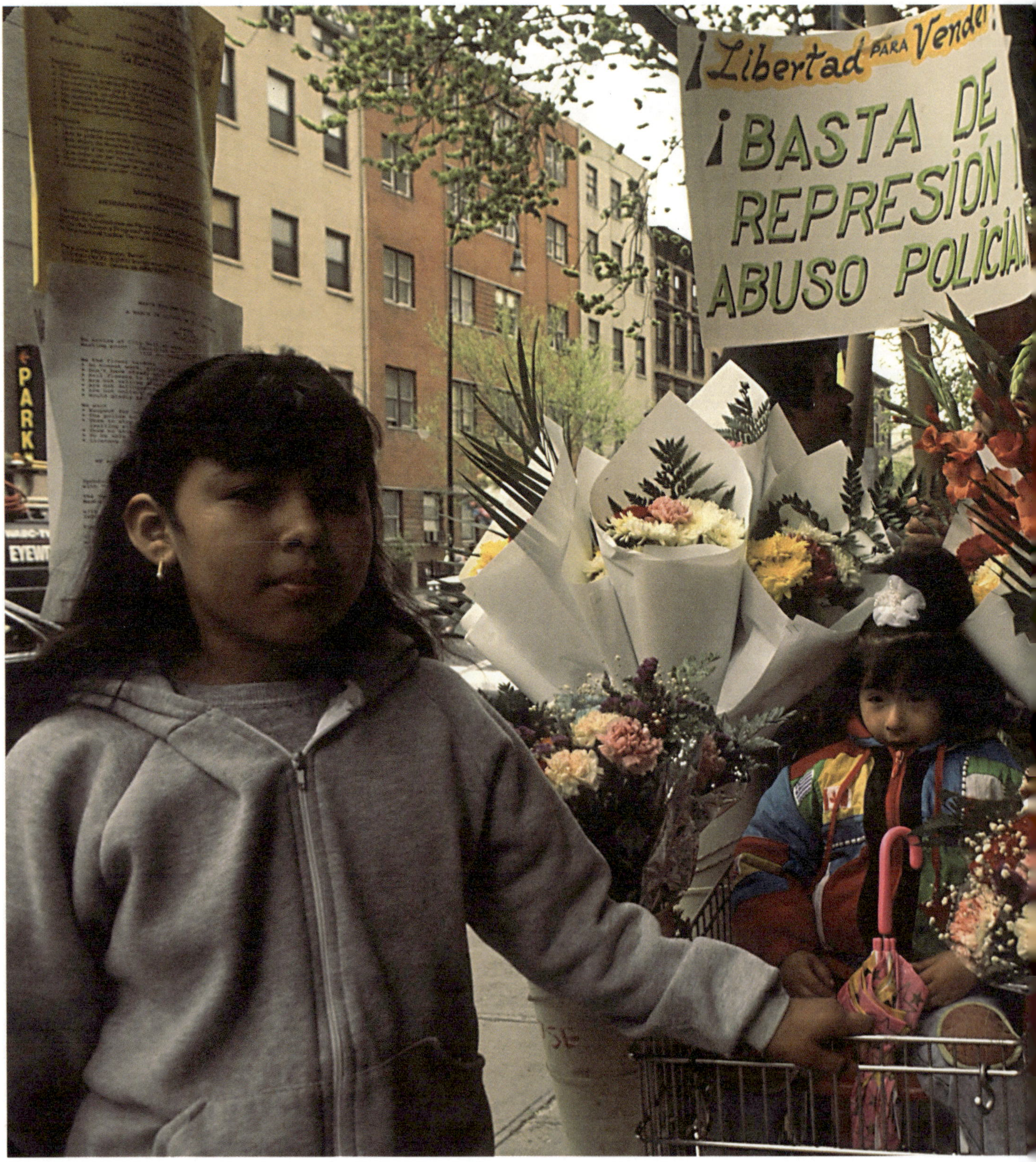
¡Libertad PARA Vender!
¡BASTA DE REPRESIÓN Y ABUSO POLICIAL!
PARK
EYEWIT

DONNA DECESARE

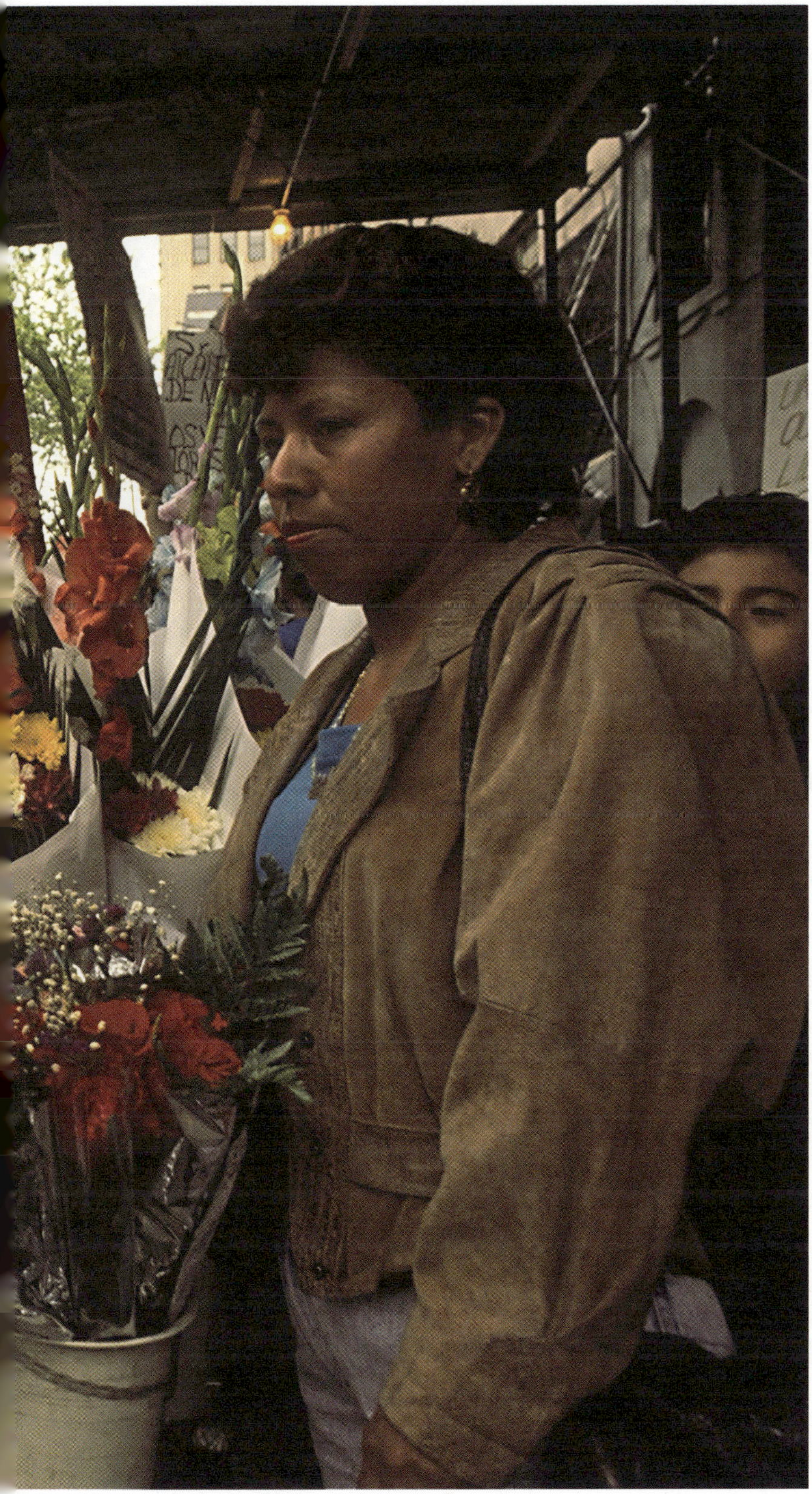

Manhattan, May 4, 1992. New York City street vendors who sell flowers, many of whom are Mexican immigrants, protest for the right to organize and to obtain licenses to legally sell their products. They are being supported by a number of unions, including the ILGWU.

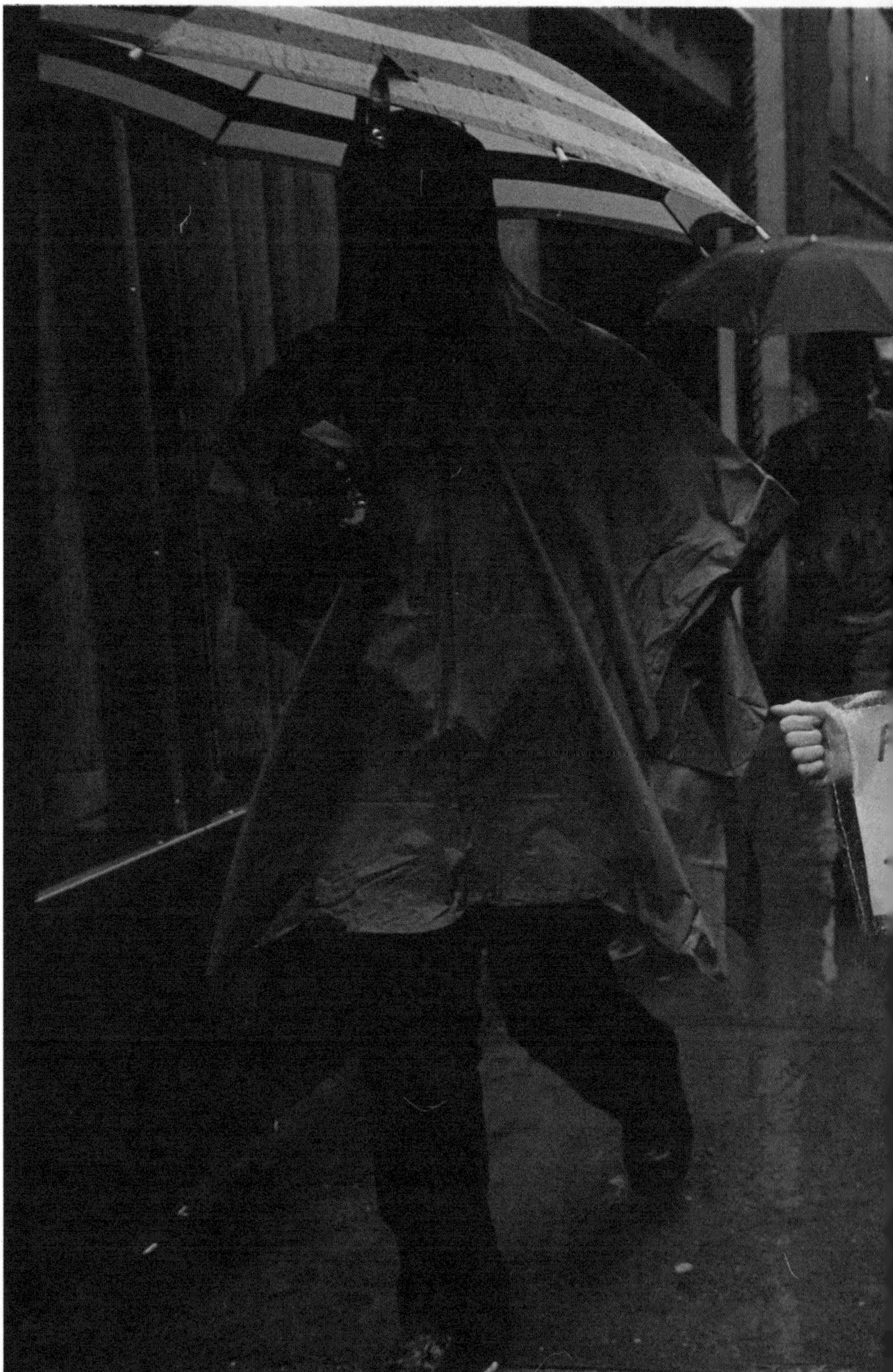

Manhattan, March 1983.
Demonstration for non-intervention
in Central America.

MAXIMO COLÓN

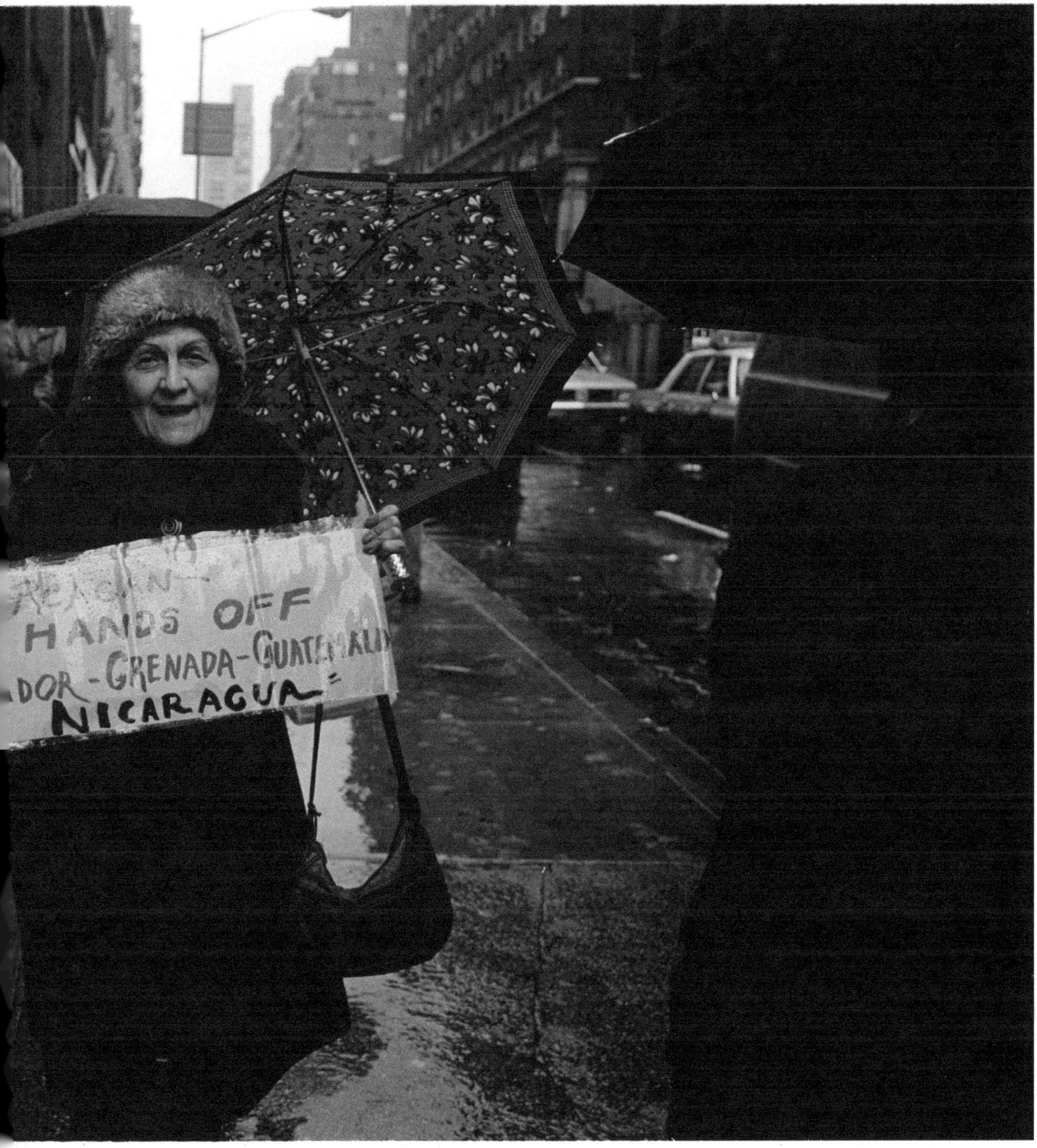

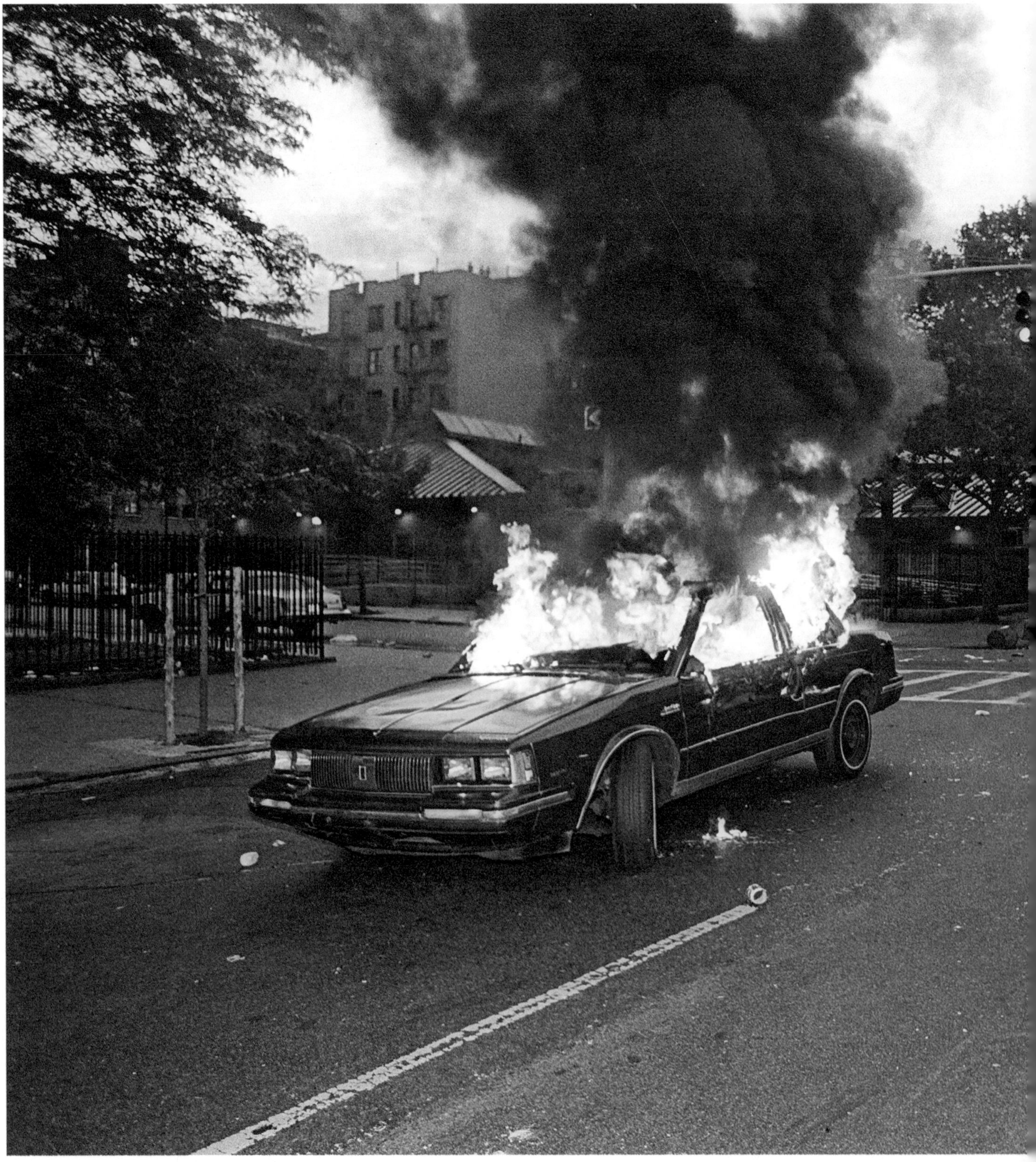

RICKY FLORES

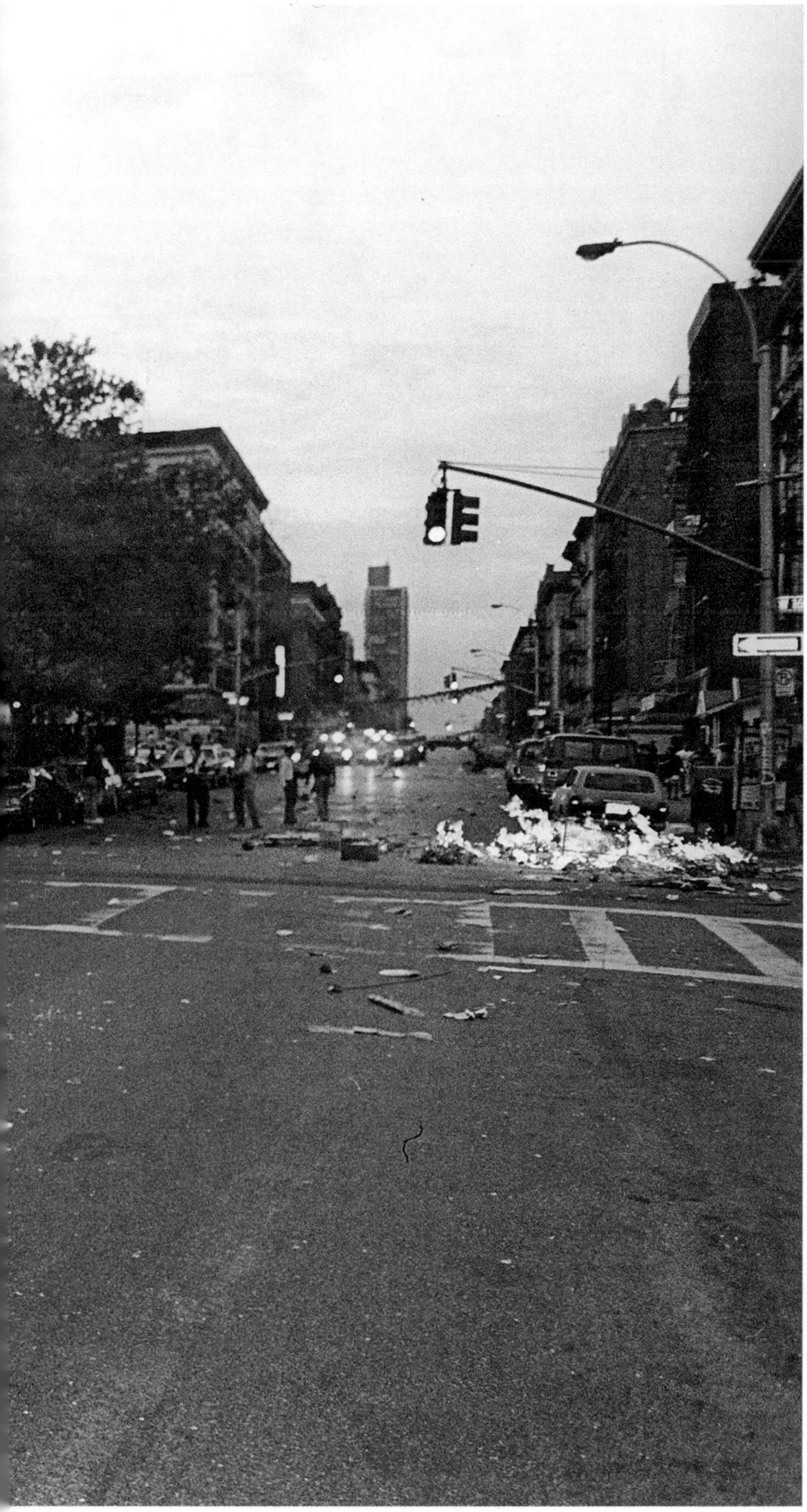

Manhattan, July, 1992. A car burns after being set on fire by demonstrators in Washington Heights in the wake of Jose "Kiko" Garcia's death. Garcia was a 23-year-old immigrant from the Dominican Republic who was shot by an undercover police officer during a neighborhood drug sweep. This was just one of the many demonstrations that took place over several days.

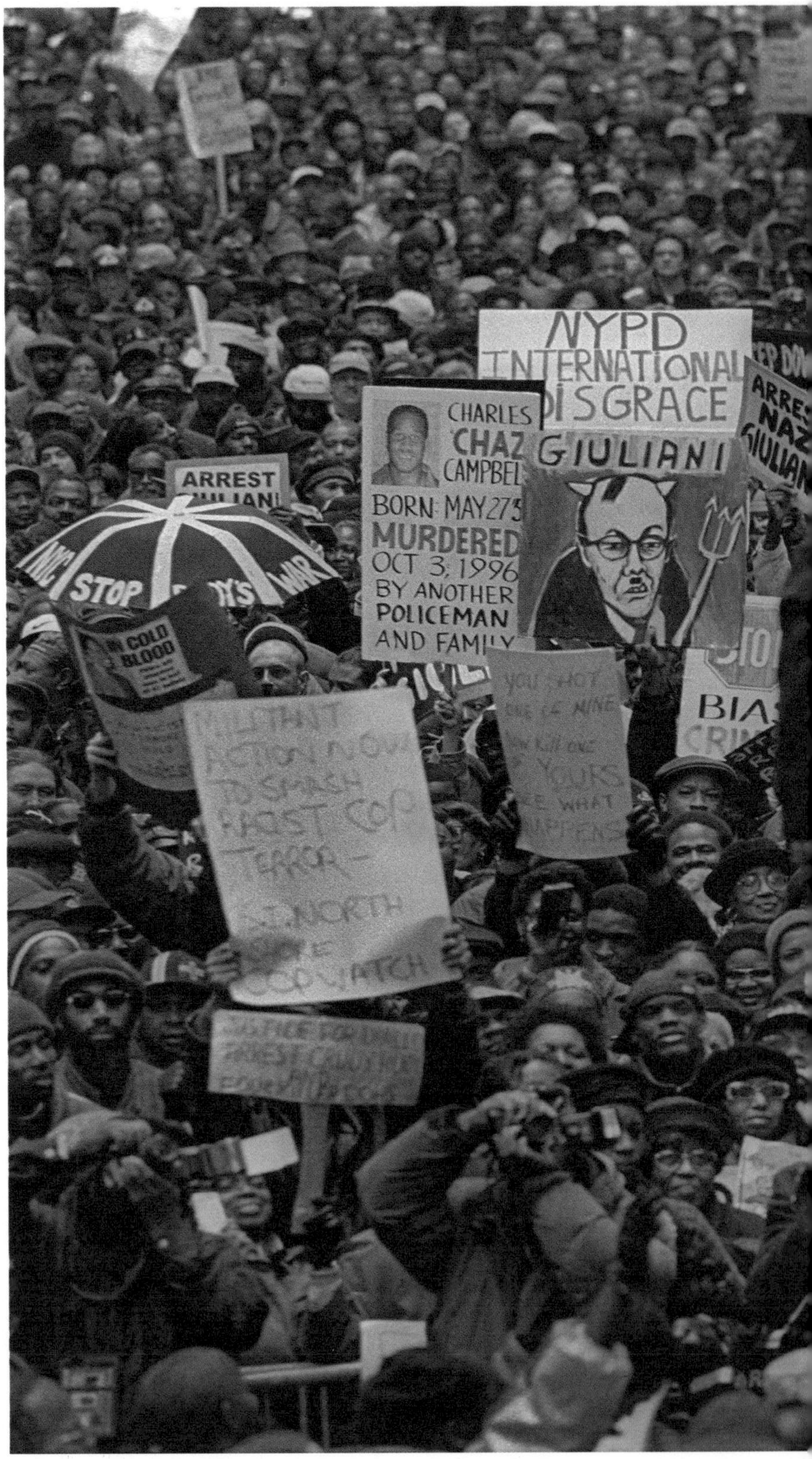

Manhattan, March, 1999. Demonstration in front of the New York Stock Exchange to demand the indictment of the four policemen who killed Amadou Diallo, a 23-year-old unarmed immigrant from Guinea.

FRANK FOURNIER

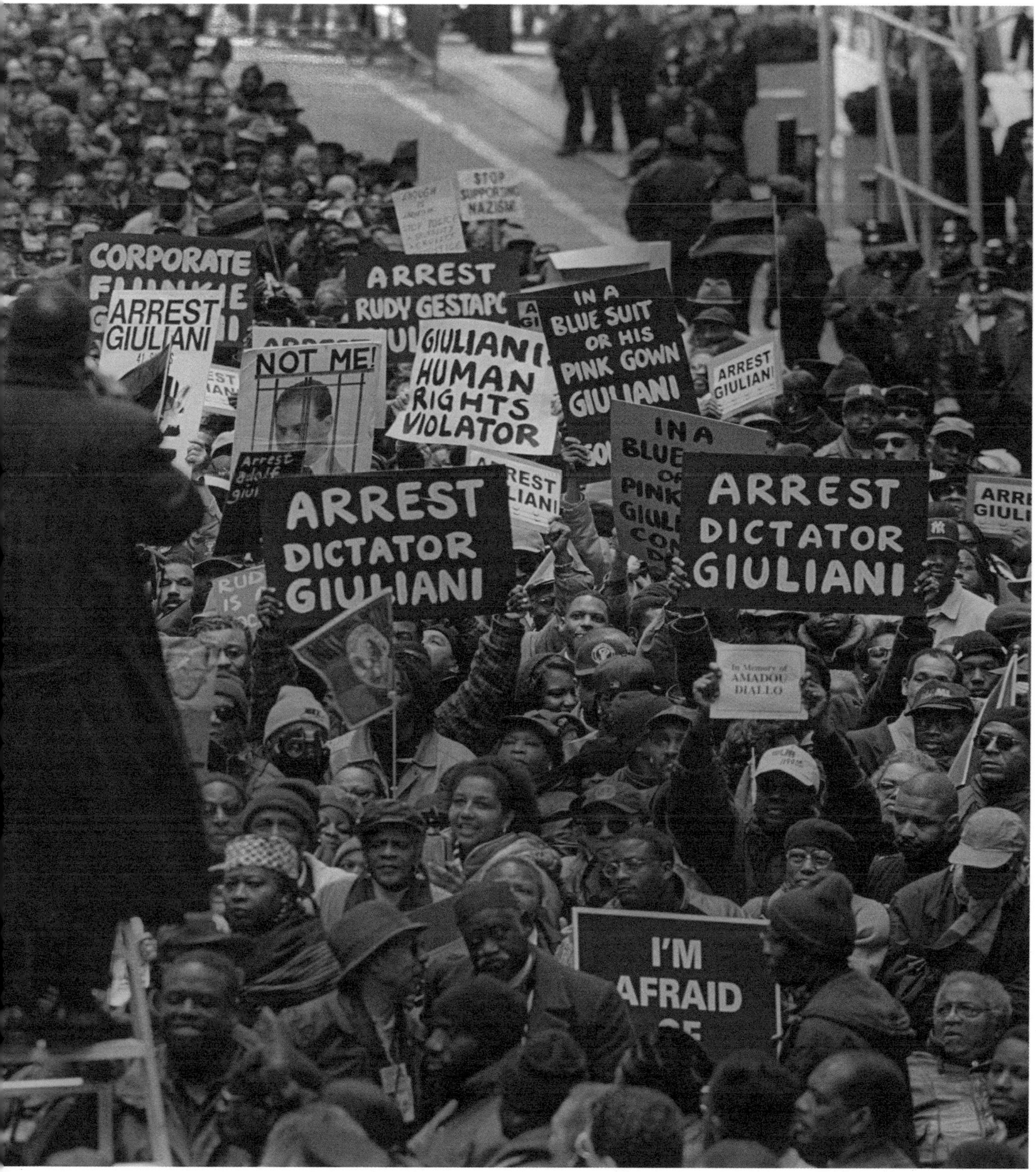

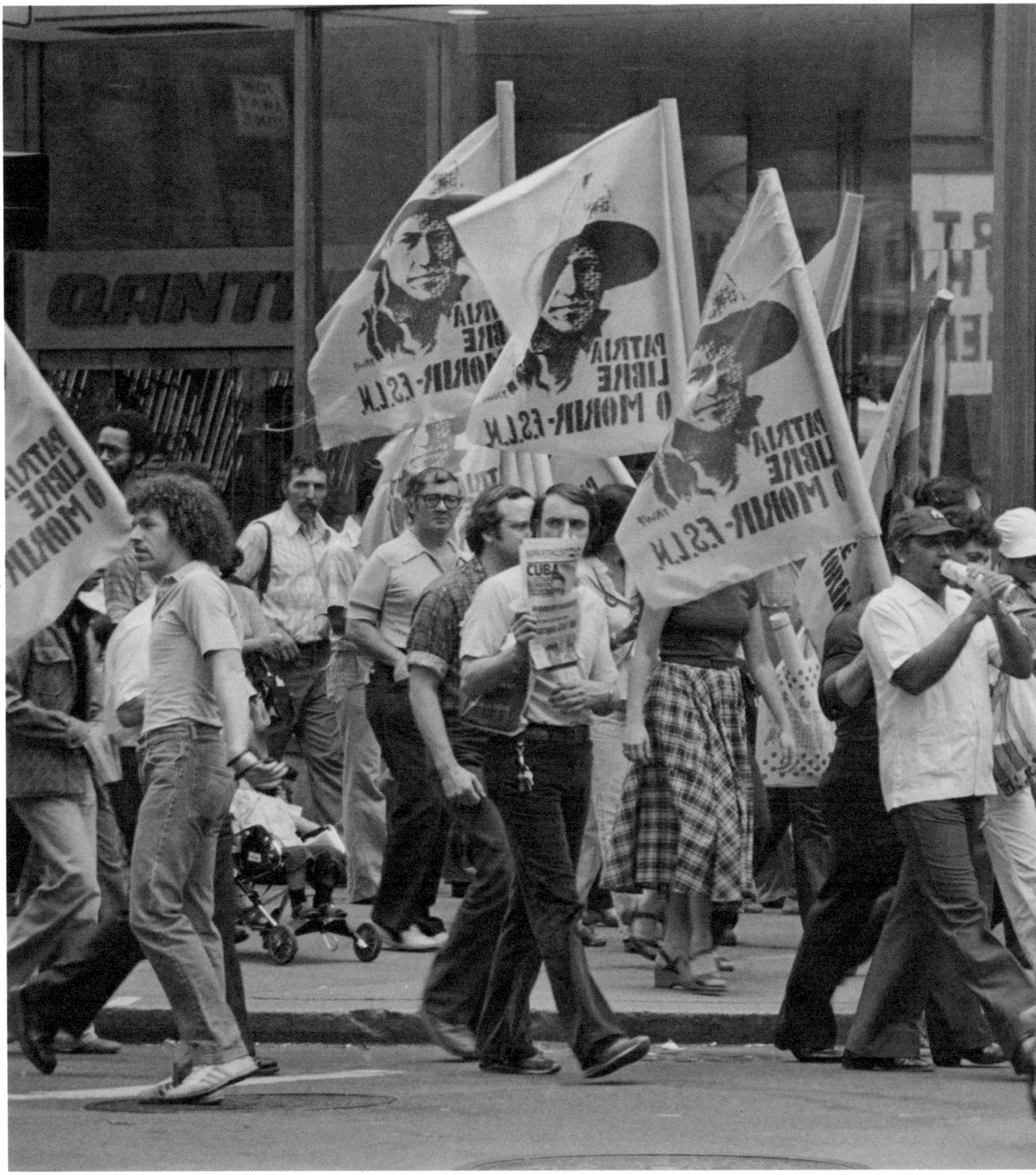
PATRIA
LIBRE
O MORIR-F.S.L.N
CUBA

DAVID GONZALEZ

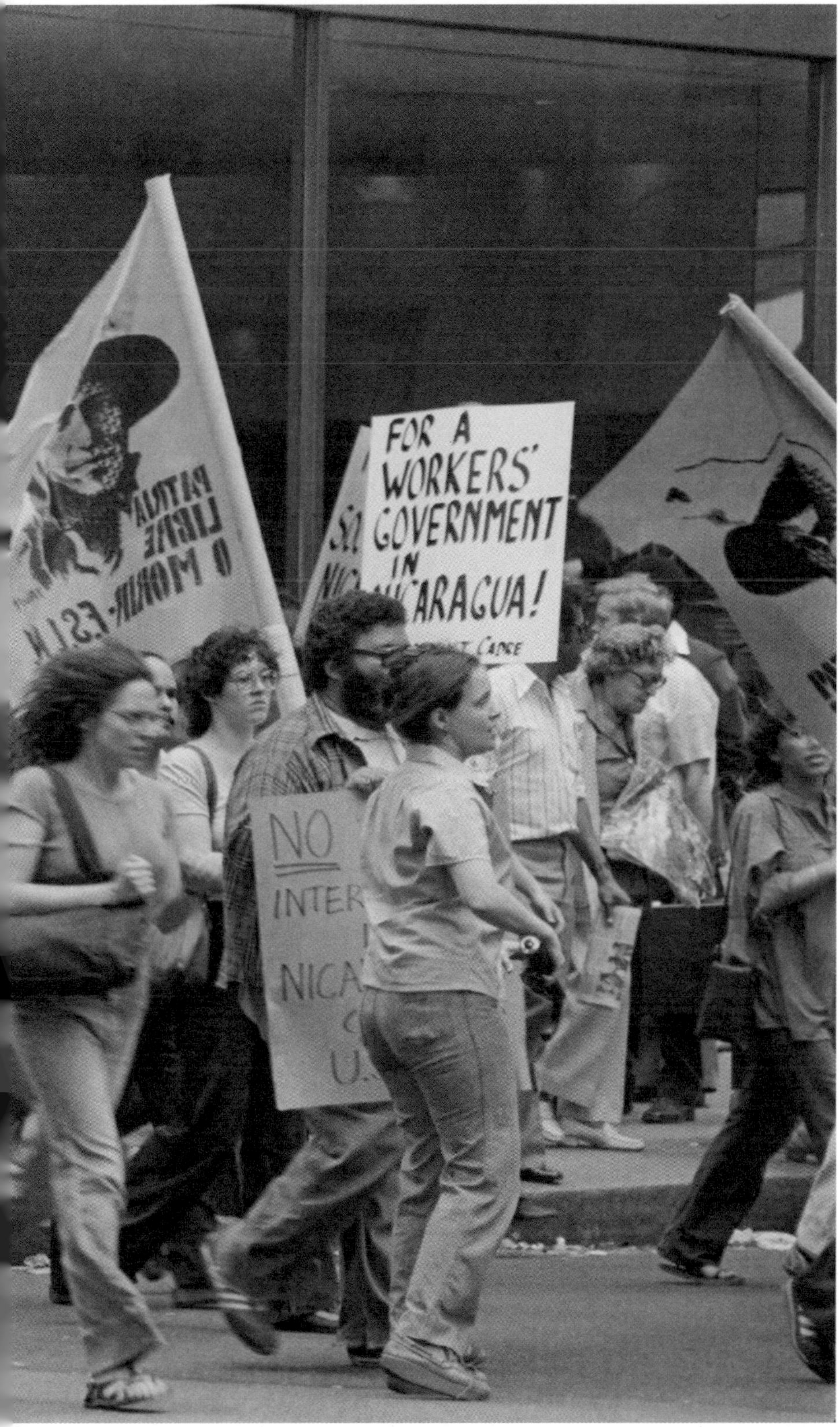

Manhattan, 1979.
Pro-Sandinista rally on 57th Street.

LORI GRINKER

Manhattan, 1985. The Guerrilla Girls, a group of radical feminist female artists, wheatpaste around New York City after midnight.

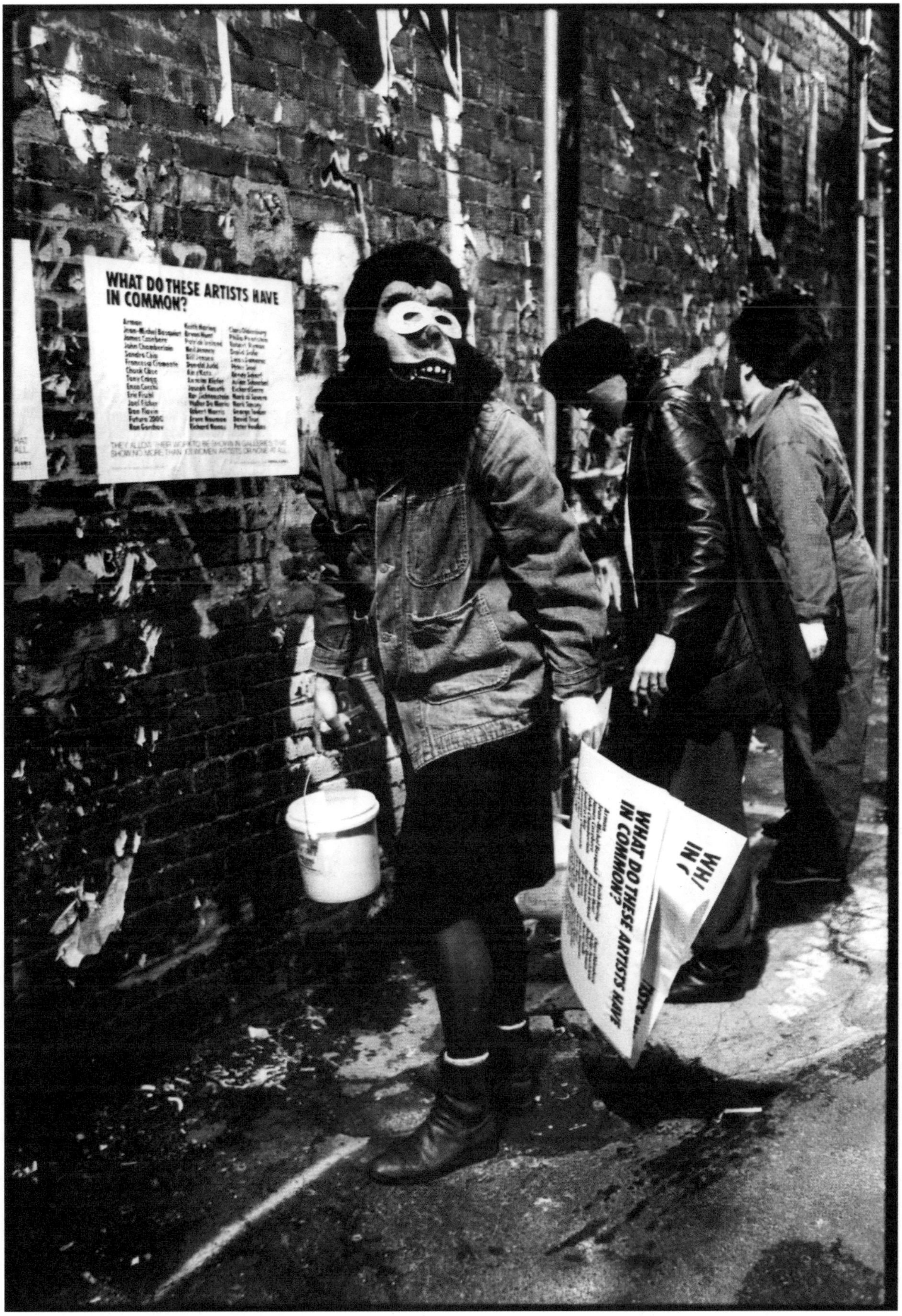
WHAT DO THESE ARTISTS HAVE IN COMMON?
WHAT DO THESE ARTISTS HAVE IN COMMON?

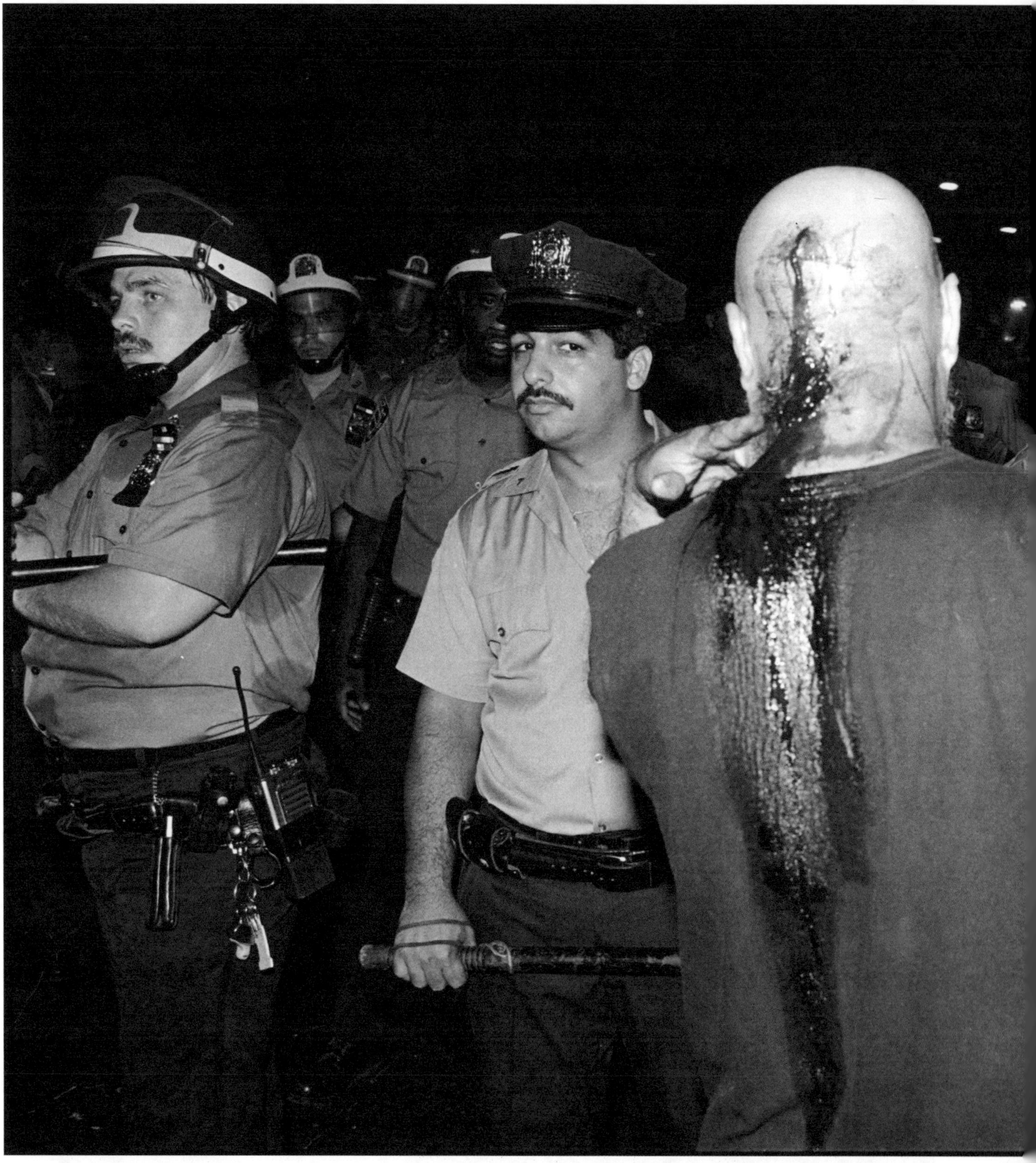

JAMES HAMILTON

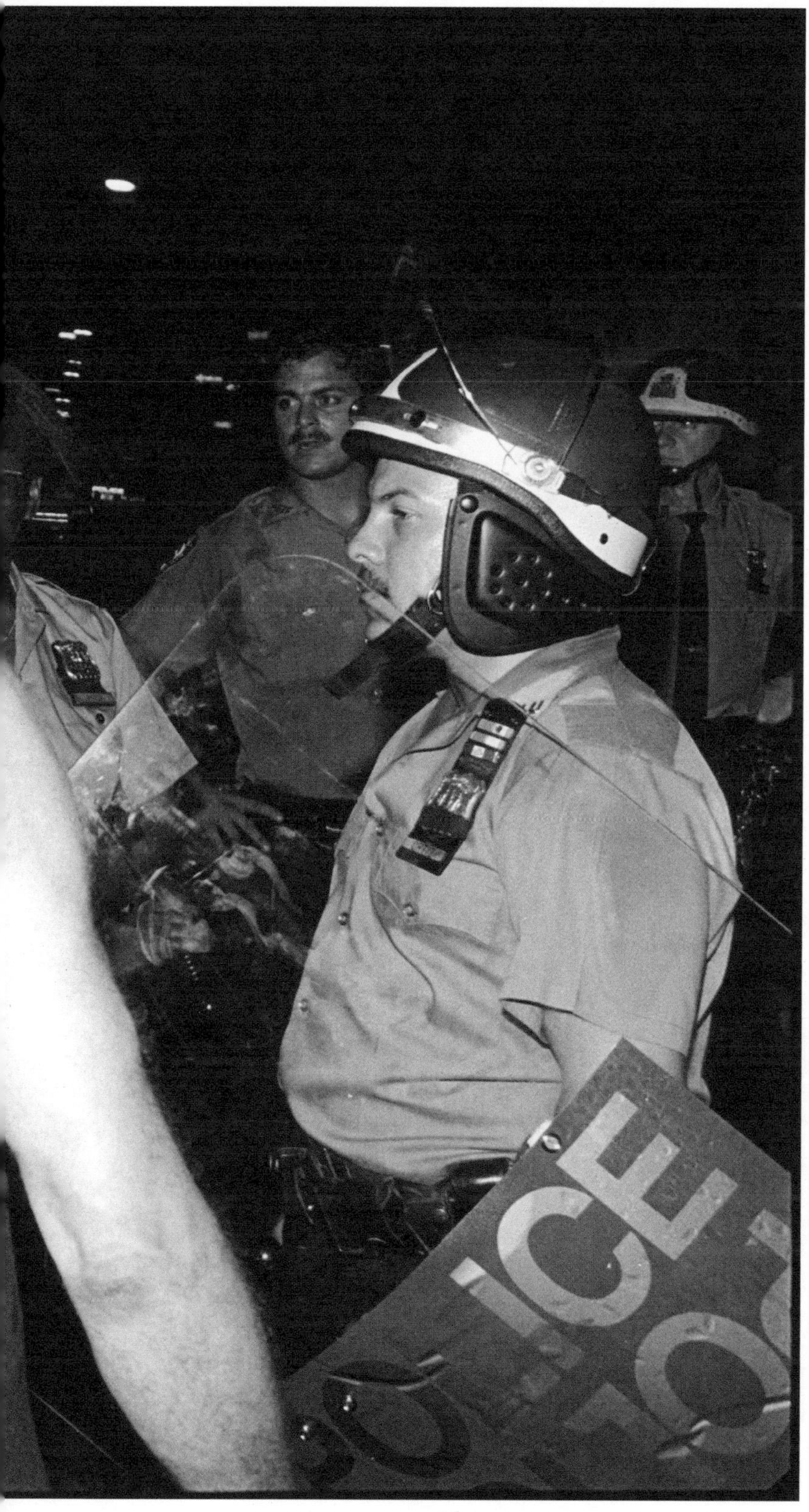

Manhattan, 1988. Tompkins Square Park riot.

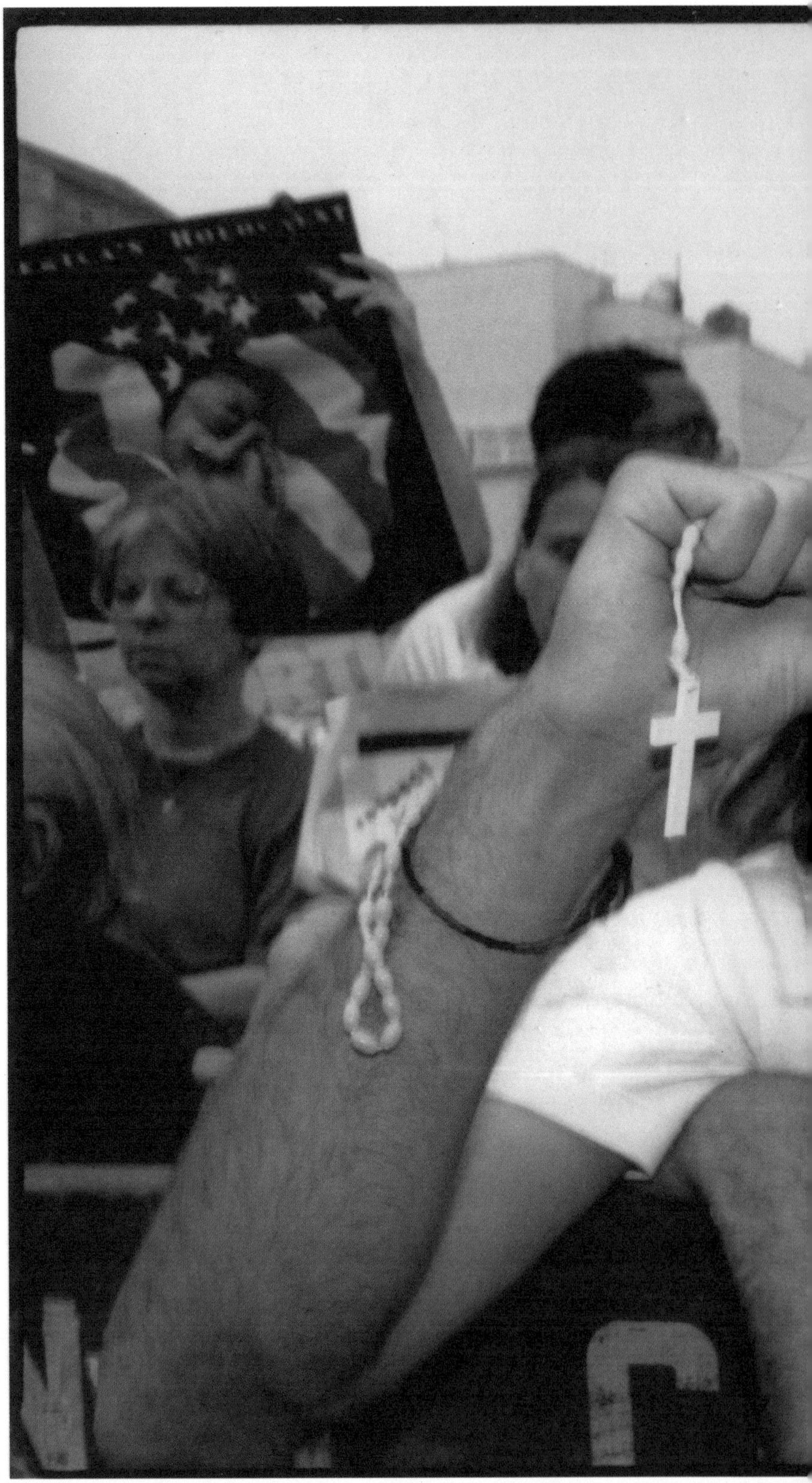

Manhattan, 1992. Operation Rescue protest outside Madison Square Garden during the Democratic National Convention.

MEG HANDLER

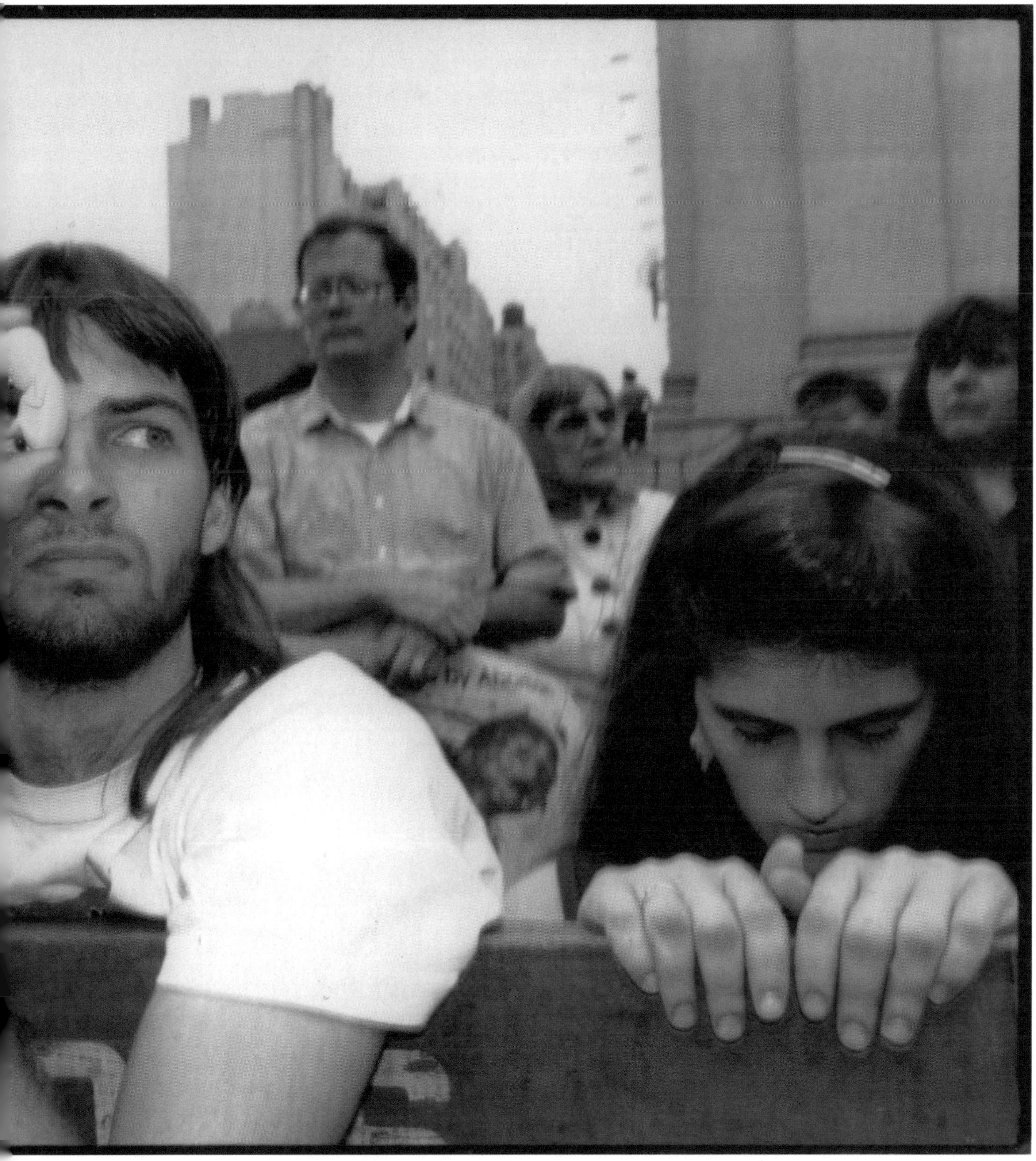

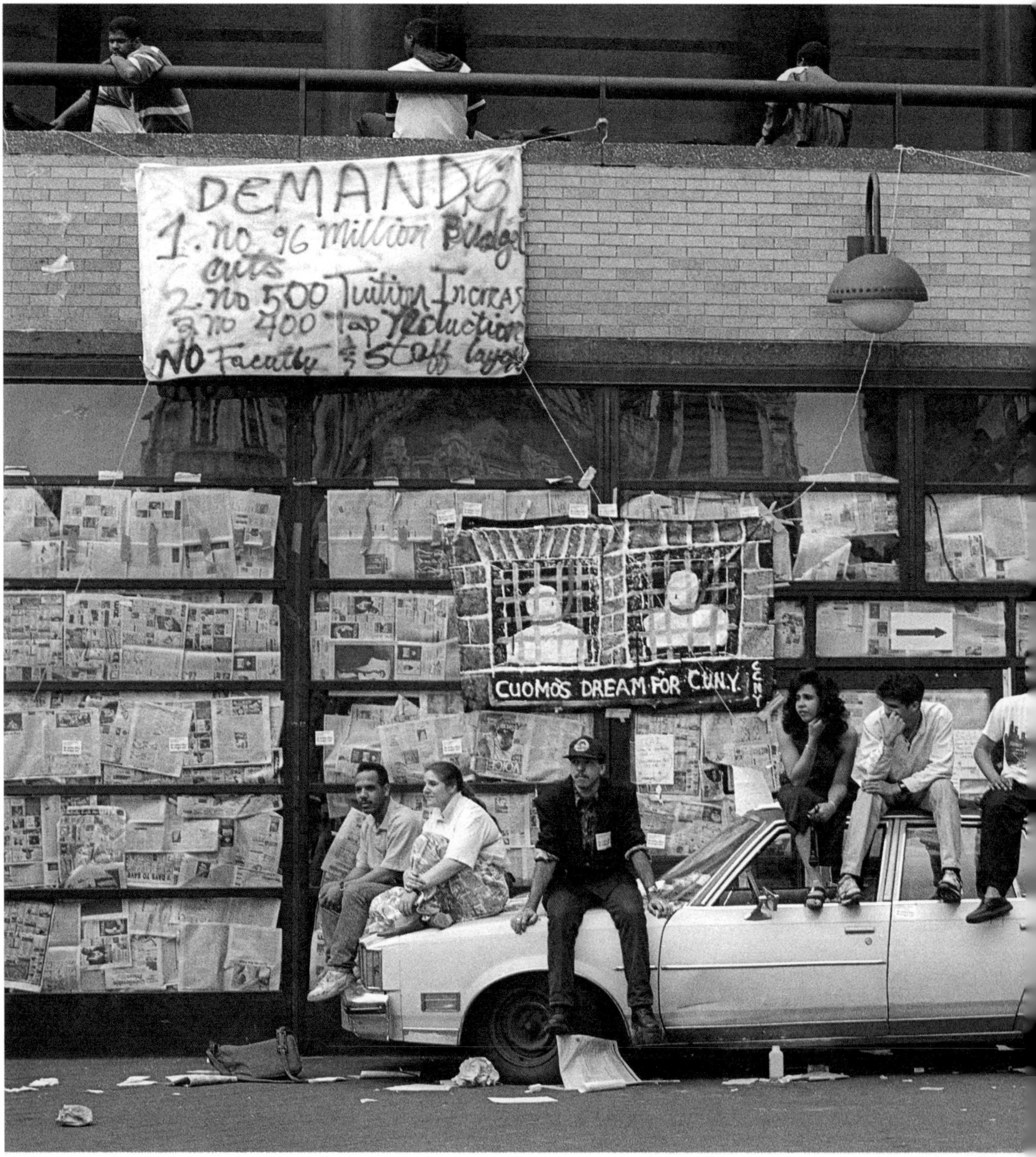
DEMANDS
1. no 96 million Budget cuts
2. no 500 Tuition Increase
3. no 400 Tap Reduction
NO Faculty & Staff layoffs
CUOMO'S DREAM FOR C.U.N.Y.
CCNY

LISA KAHANE

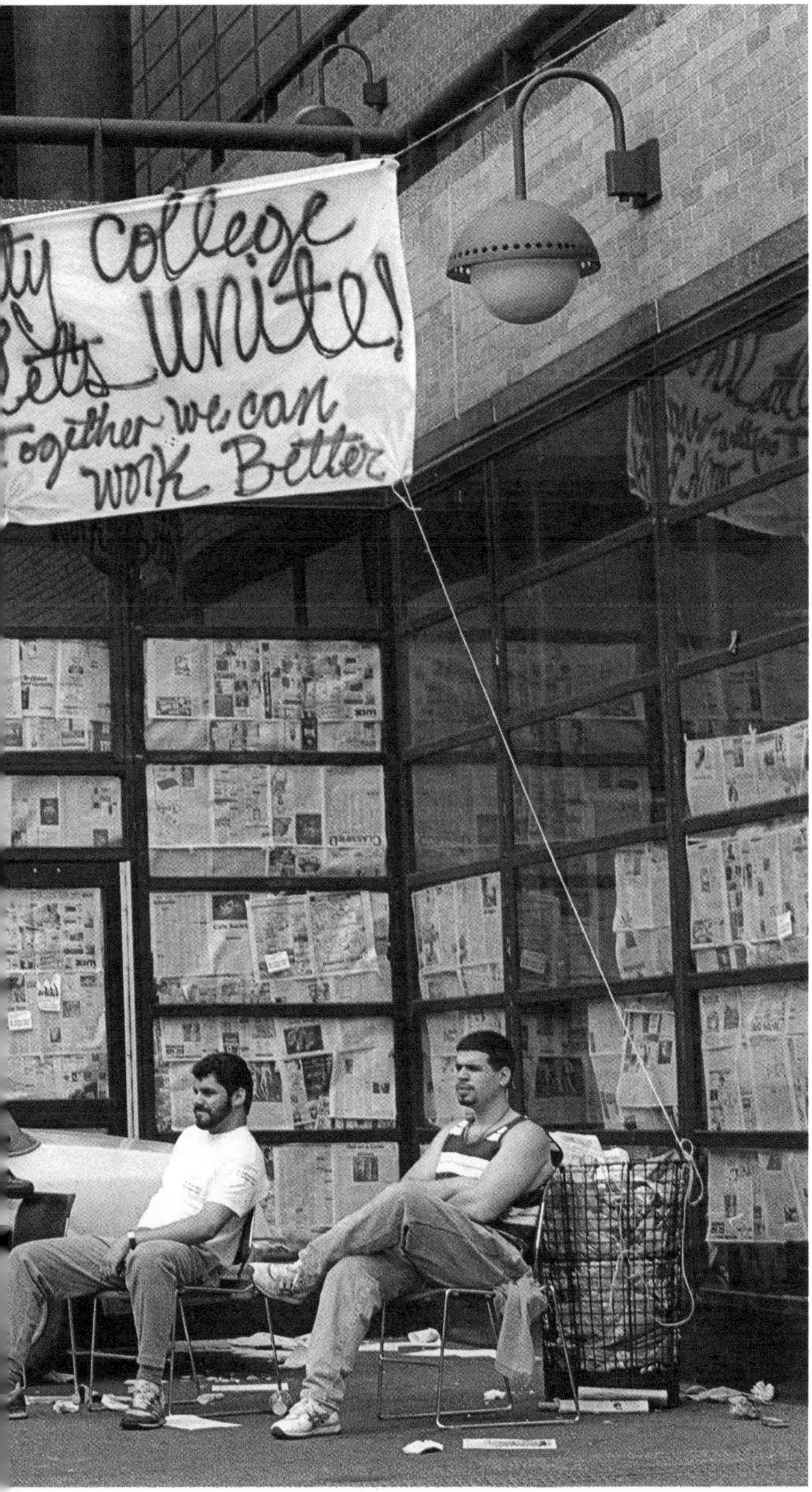

Manhattan, April 9, 1991. Students sit on a parked car outside an occupied building on the City College campus during the CUNY student strike against proposed tuition hikes and budget cuts.

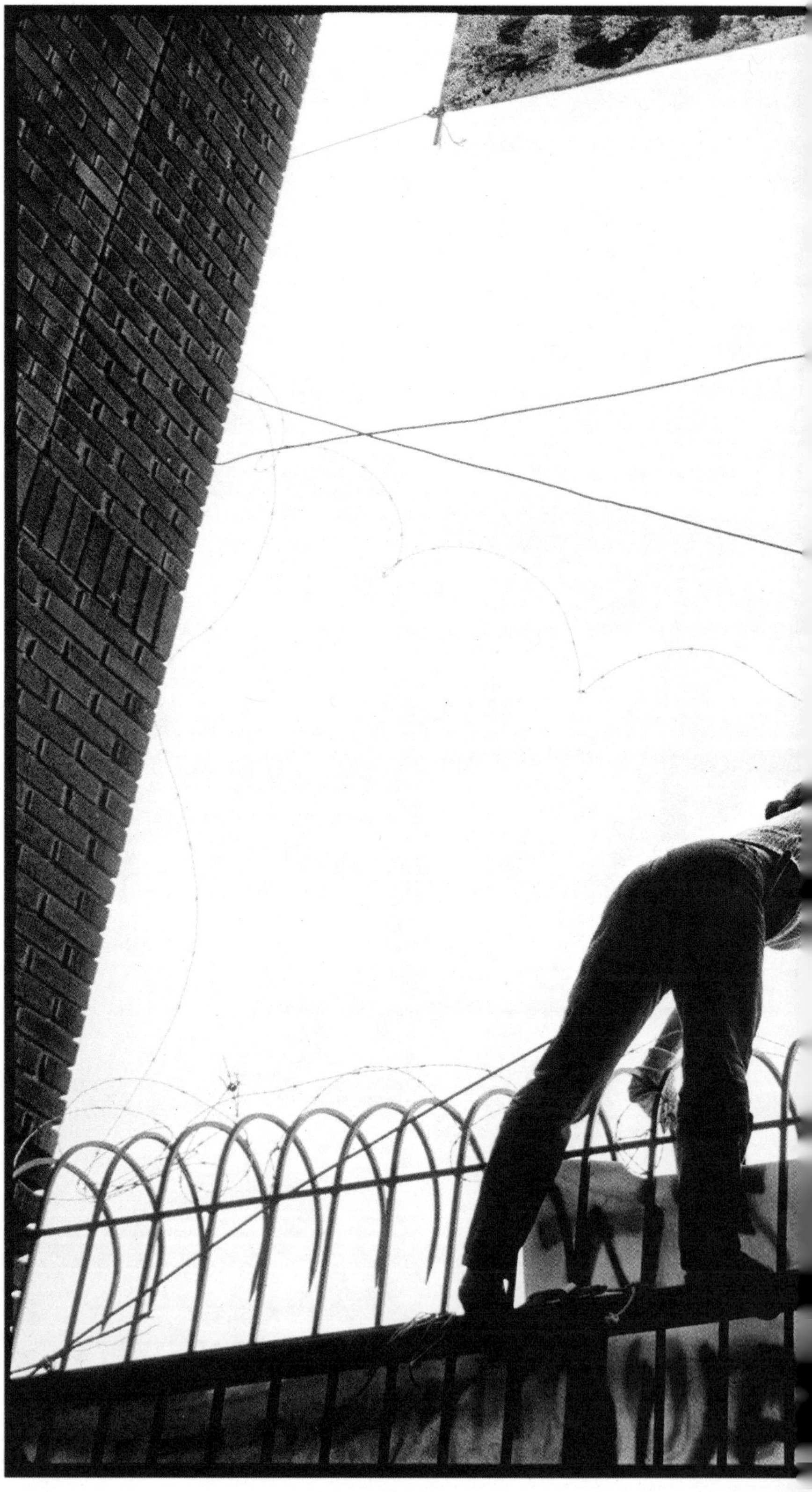

Bronx, 1988. Tenants and supporters demonstrate and barricade against eviction by New York City marshals. The tenants, mostly low income New Yorkers and artists, took over the abandoned building on Cypress Avenue and invested tens of thousands of dollars and several years of sweat equity, replacing the roof, boiler and other building infrastructure. The city sold the building to a developer who eventually evicted the families.

MIKE KAMBER

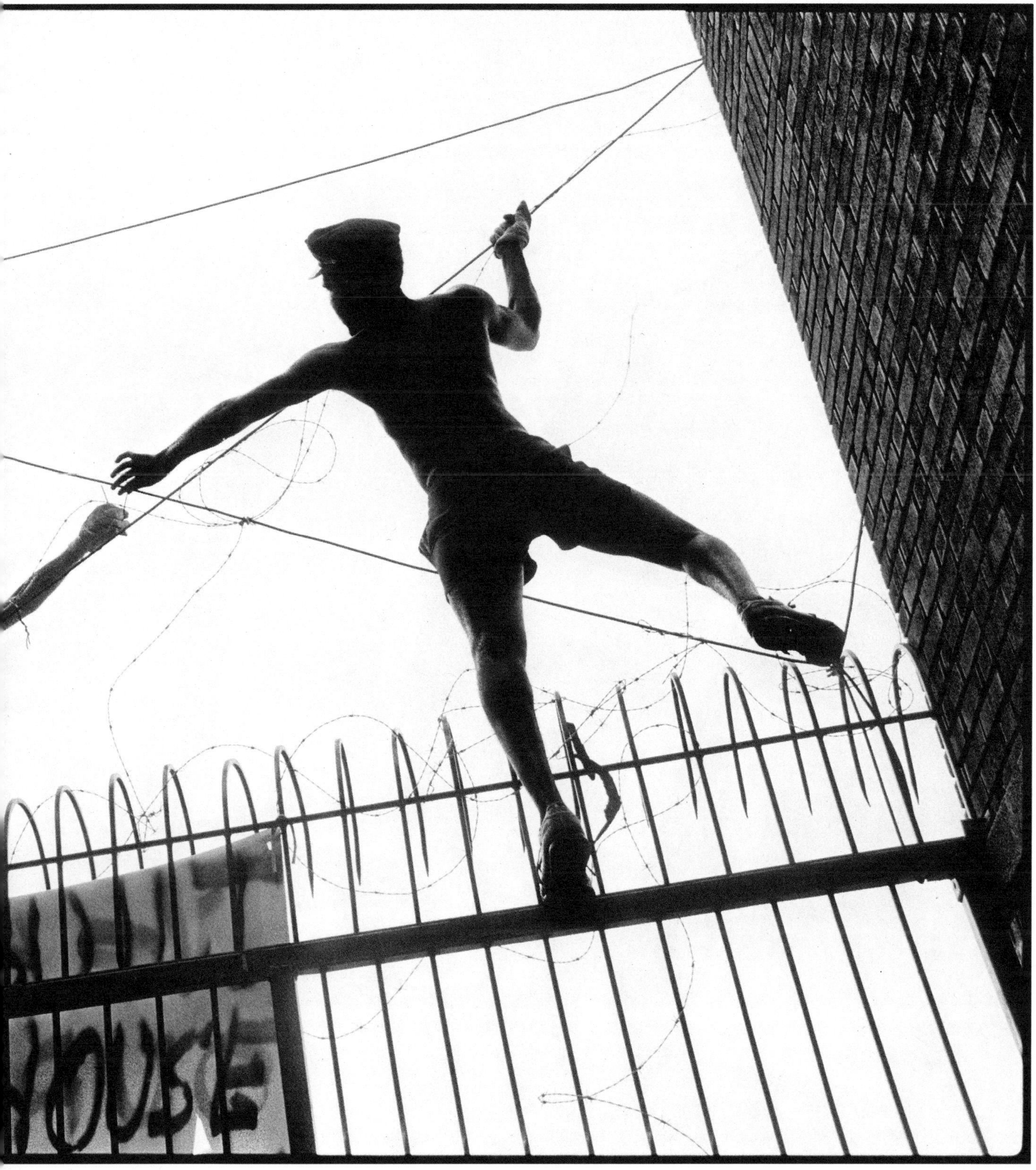

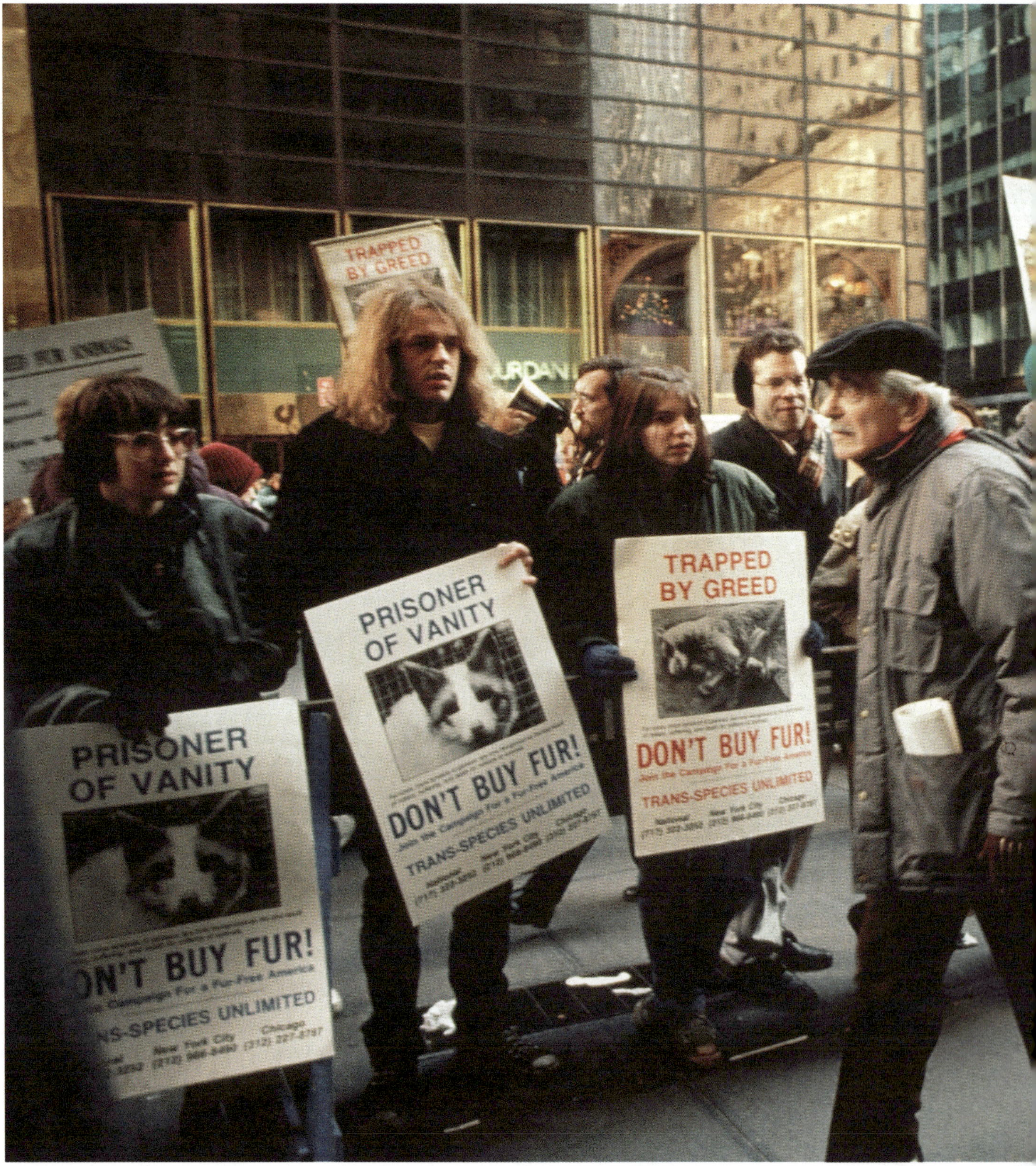
TRAPPED BY GREED
PRISONER OF VANITY
DON'T BUY FUR!
Join the Campaign For a Fur-Free America
TRANS-SPECIES UNLIMITED

GABE KIRCHHEIMER

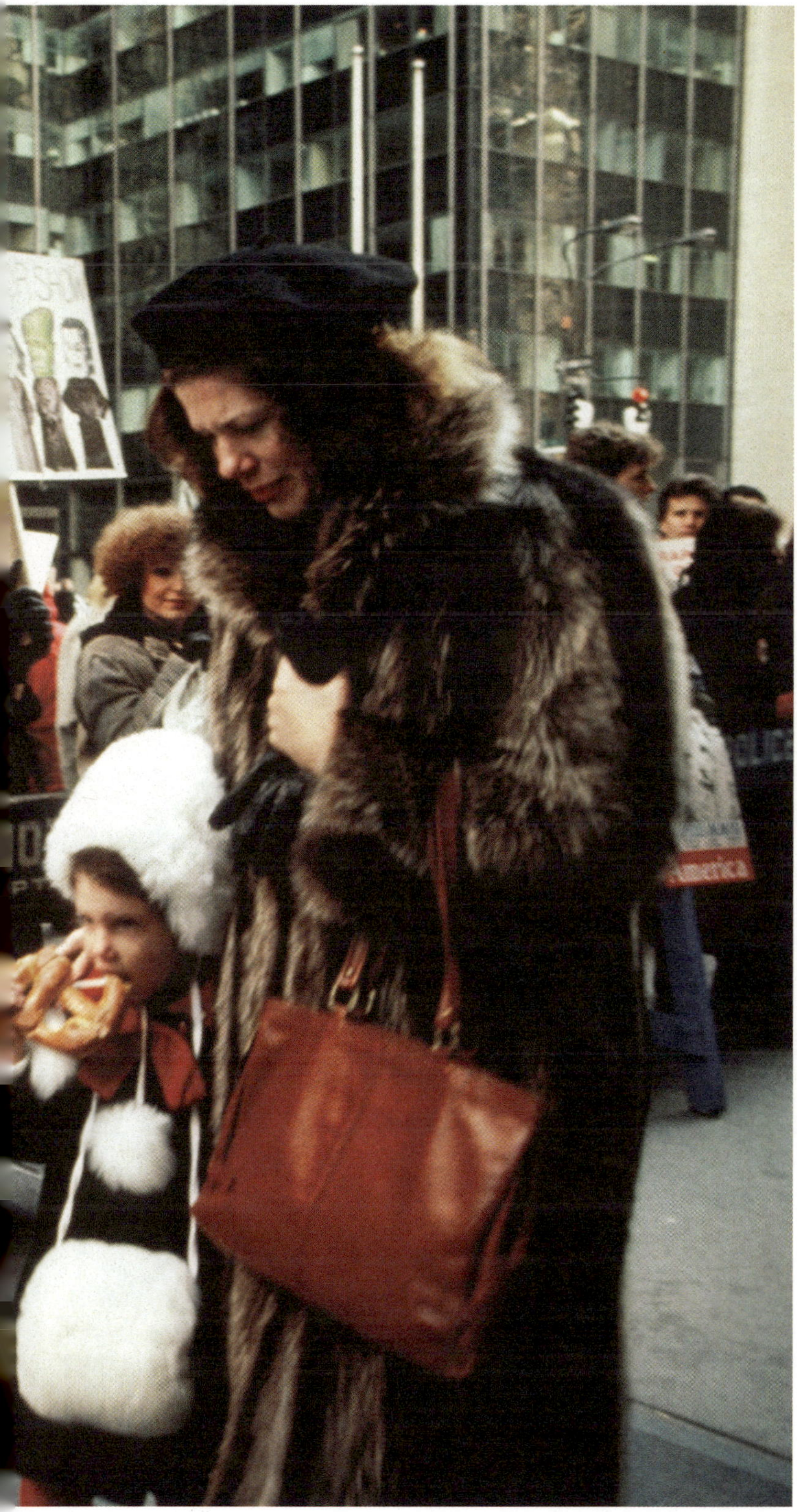

Manhattan, 1989. A woman in a fur coat walks past anti-fur protesters on 5th Avenue, across the street from Trump Tower.

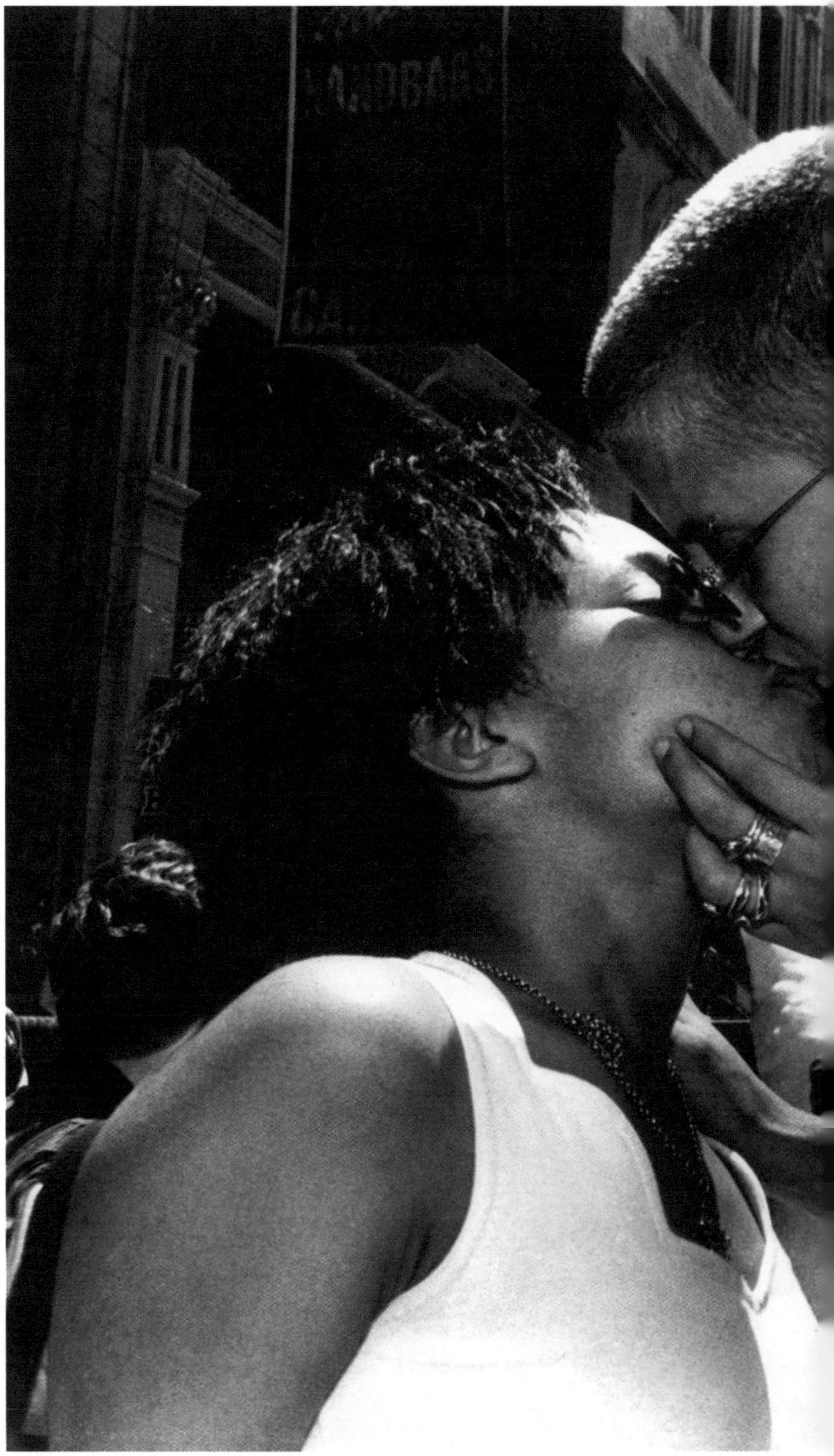

Manhattan, 1993. Members of the Lesbian Avengers, a direct action and visibility group, begin their first annual Dyke March, a tradition that has spread to cities around the world and lasts to this day.

CAROLINA KROON

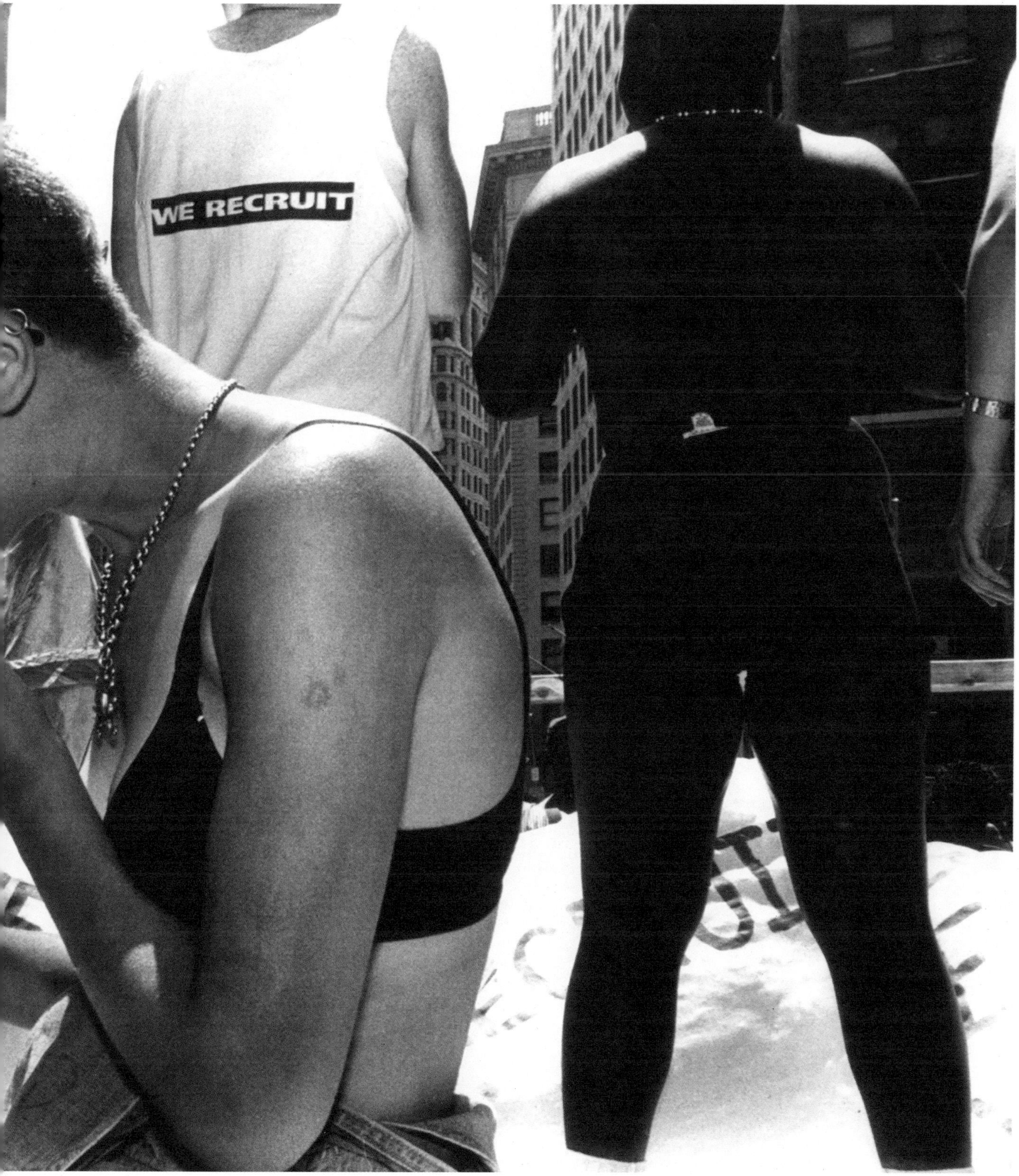

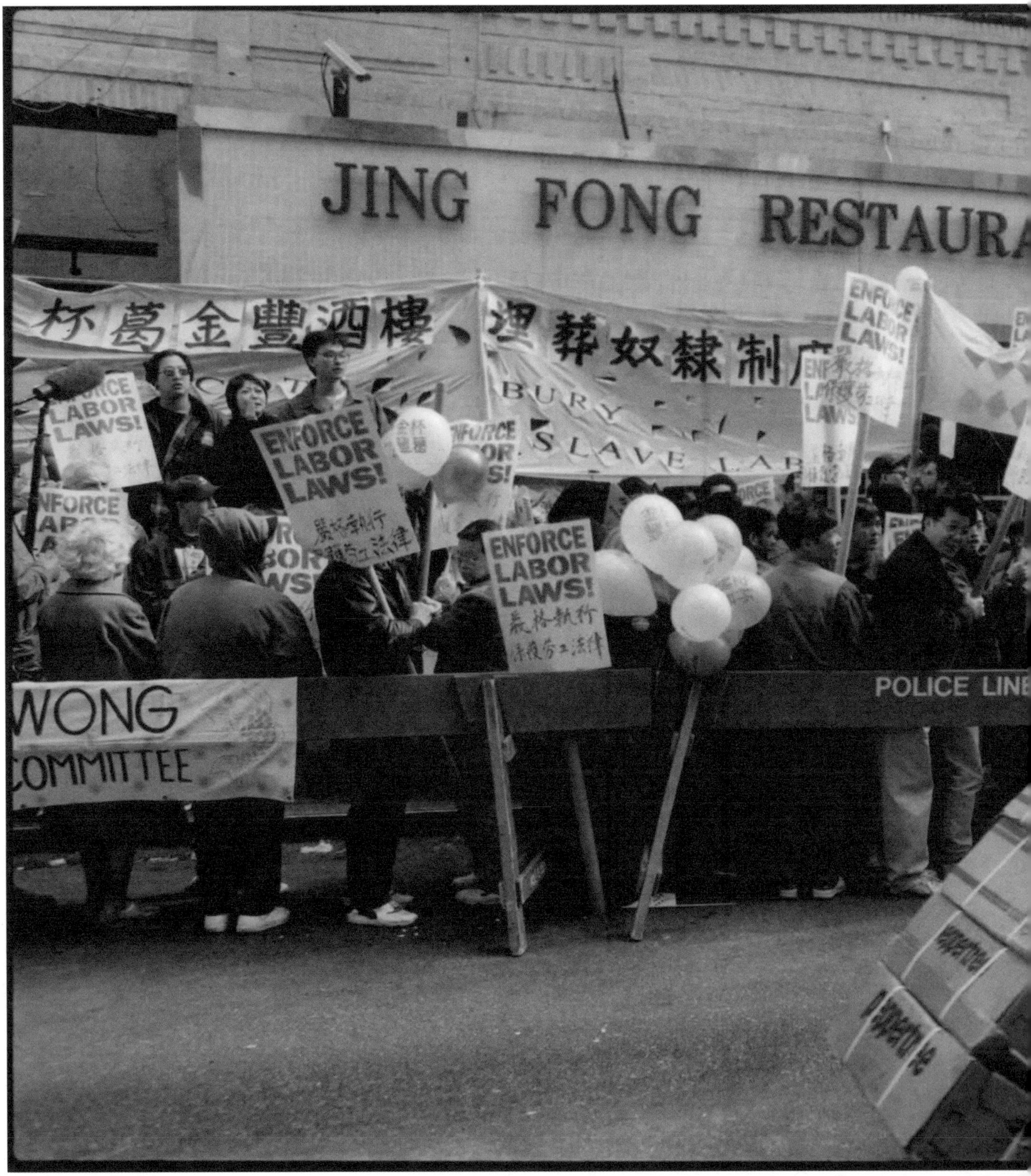
JING FONG RESTAURA
杯葛金豐酒樓、埋葬奴隸制
BURY
SLAVE
ENFORCE LABOR LAWS!
ENFORCE LABOR LAWS!
嚴格執行
保護勞工法律
POLICE LIN
WONG
COMMITTEE

CORKY LEE

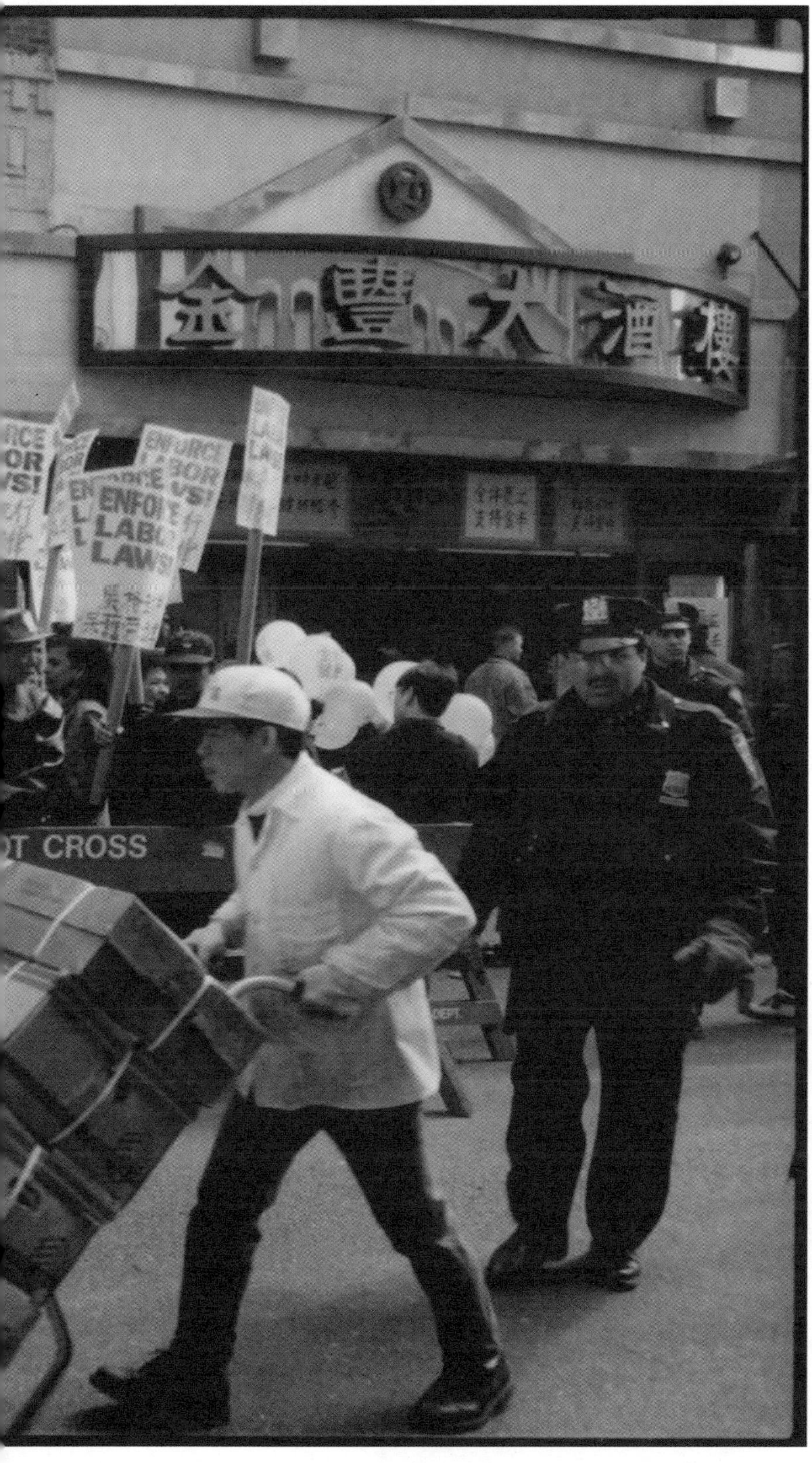

Manhattan, 1995. Fired workers and community supporters picket Jing Fong Restaurant in Chinatown, the largest facility in the community; workers claimed the restaurant management stole waiters' tips. In 1995, the NY State Attorney General sided with the workers and fined the restaurant $1.13 million in back wages.

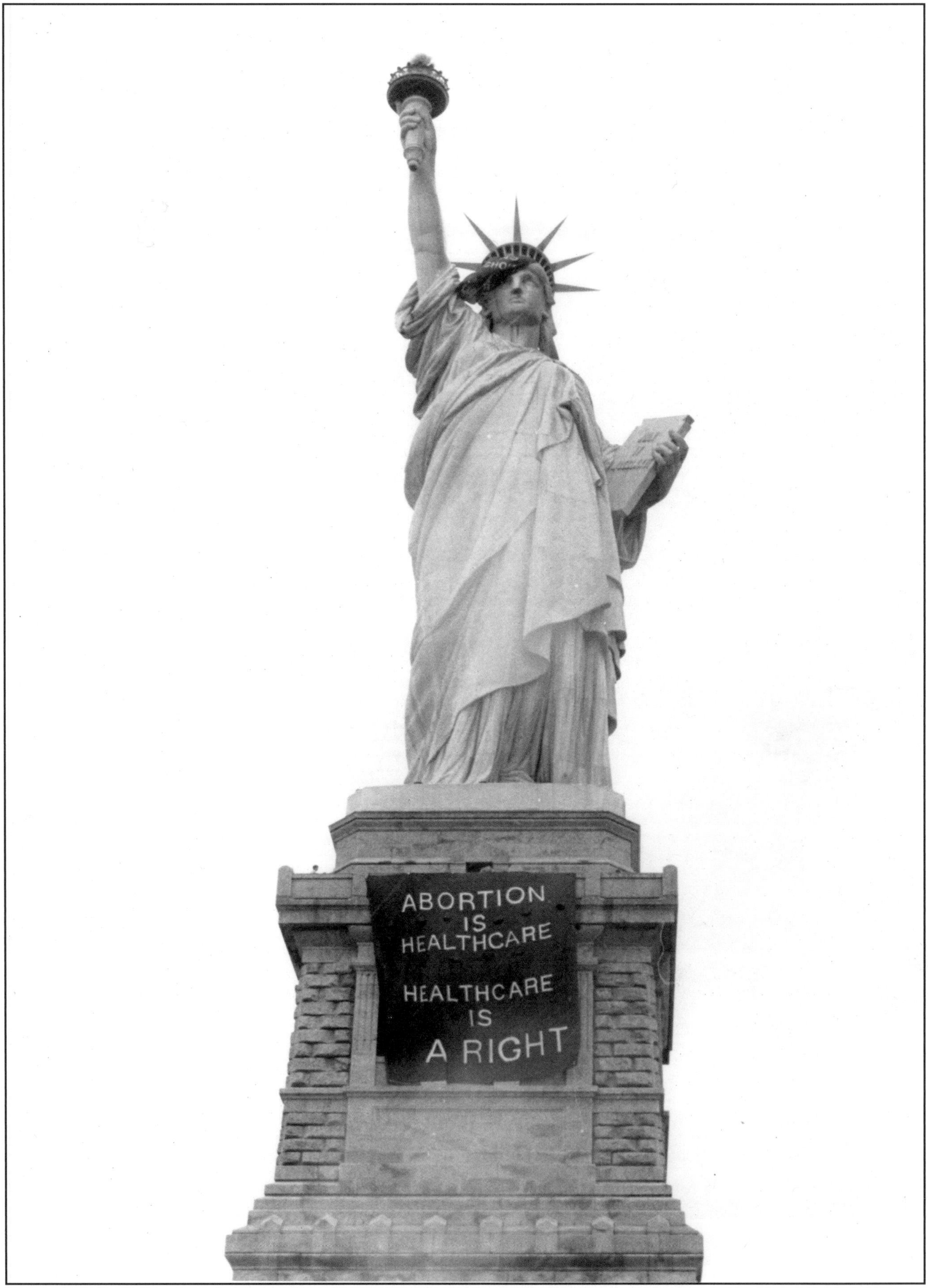
ABORTION
IS
HEALTHCARE
HEALTHCARE
IS
A RIGHT

MERYL LEVIN

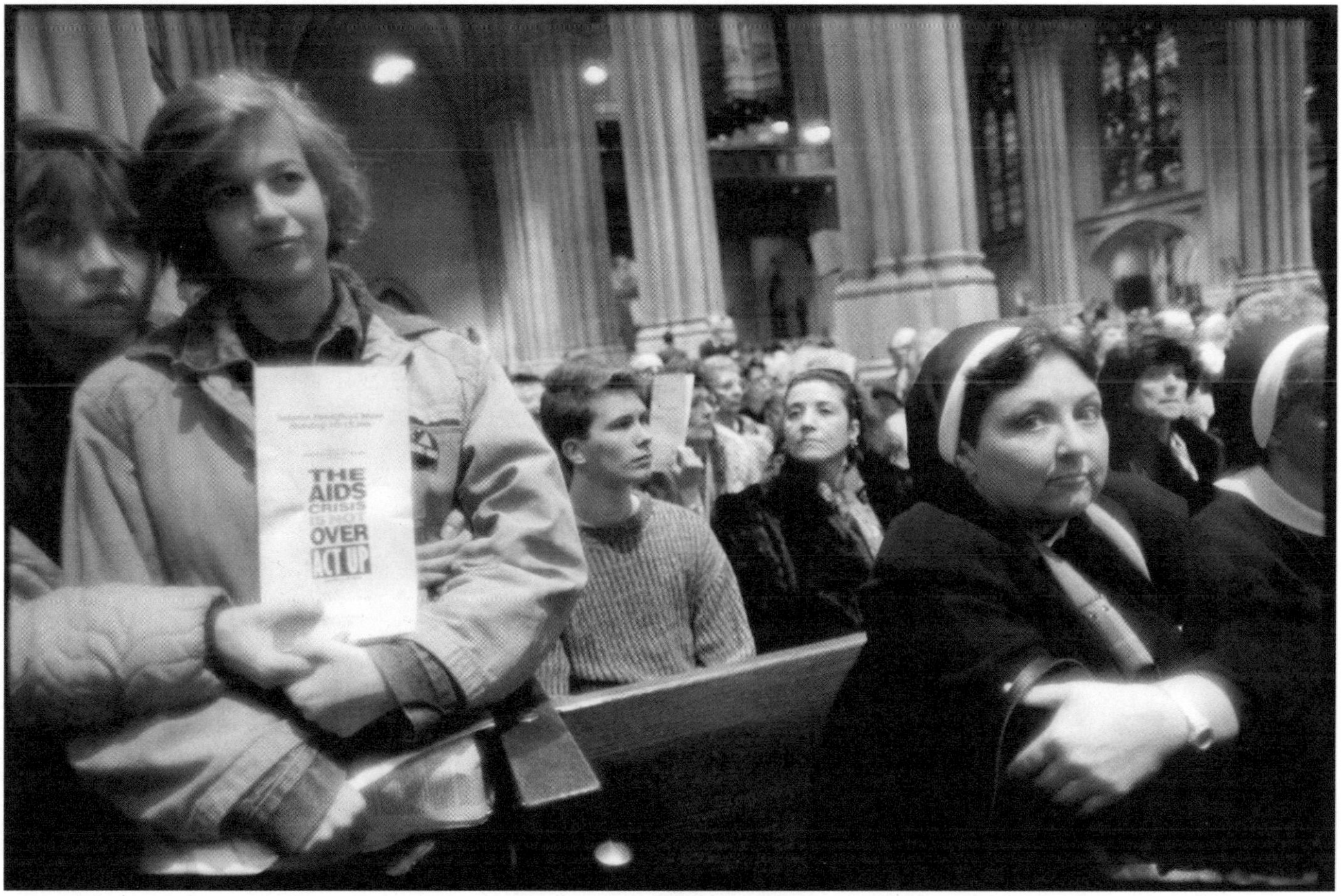

[ABOVE] Manhattan, 1990. Members of ACT UP and WHAM! protest the Catholic Church's policies on homosexuality and safe sex education as the AIDS epidemic raged on. Protesters inside the church stood silently, displaying signs and ACT UP literature, as others chanted.

[LEFT] Manhattan, 1991. Members of WHAM! and ACT UP joined forces at the Statue of Liberty to bring attention to safe and legal abortion access as a women's health care issue.

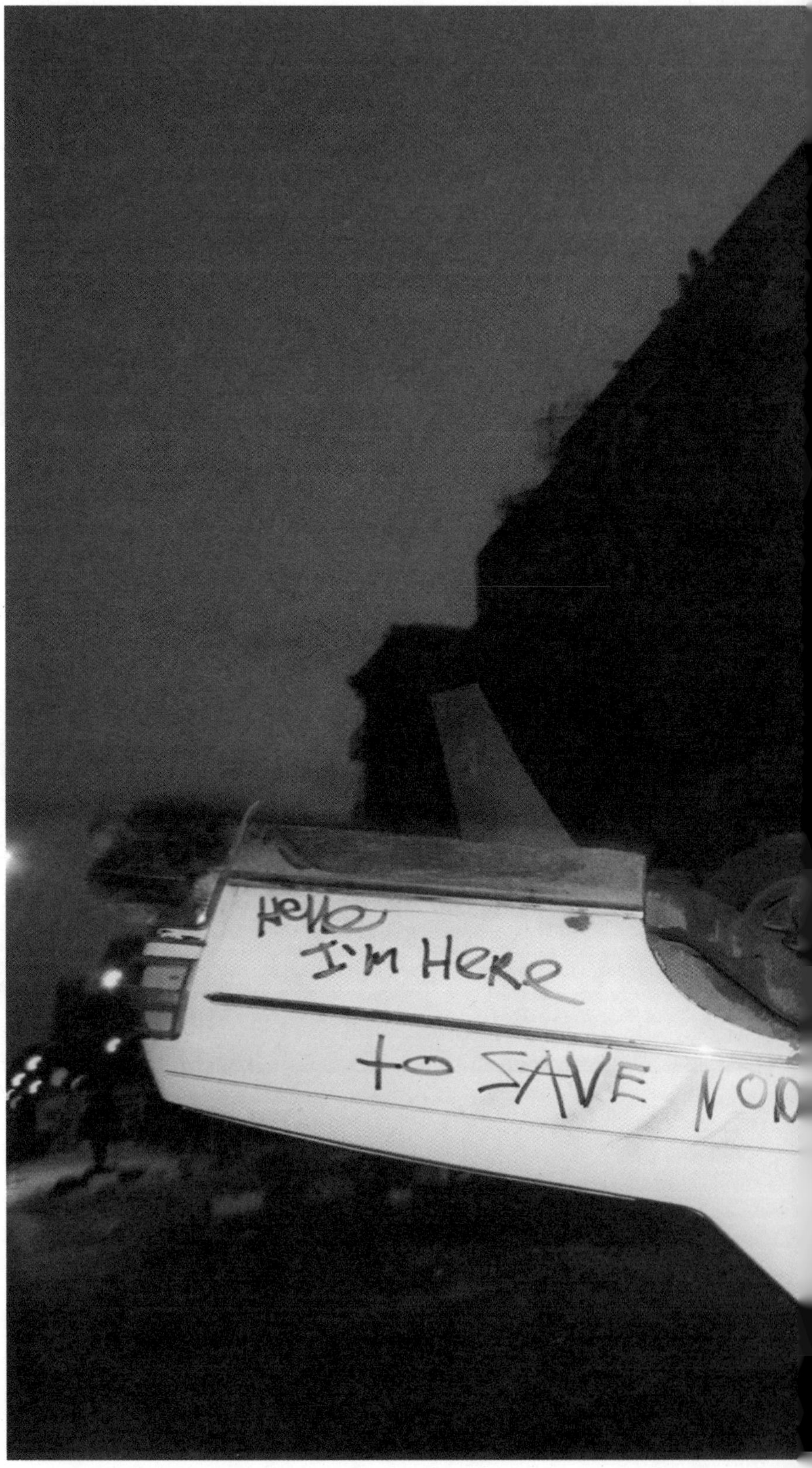

Manhattan, 1995. Squatters attempt to defend their building from an expected attack by the police on East 13th Street by blocking the street with overturned cars and trash.

ANDREW LICHTENSTEIN

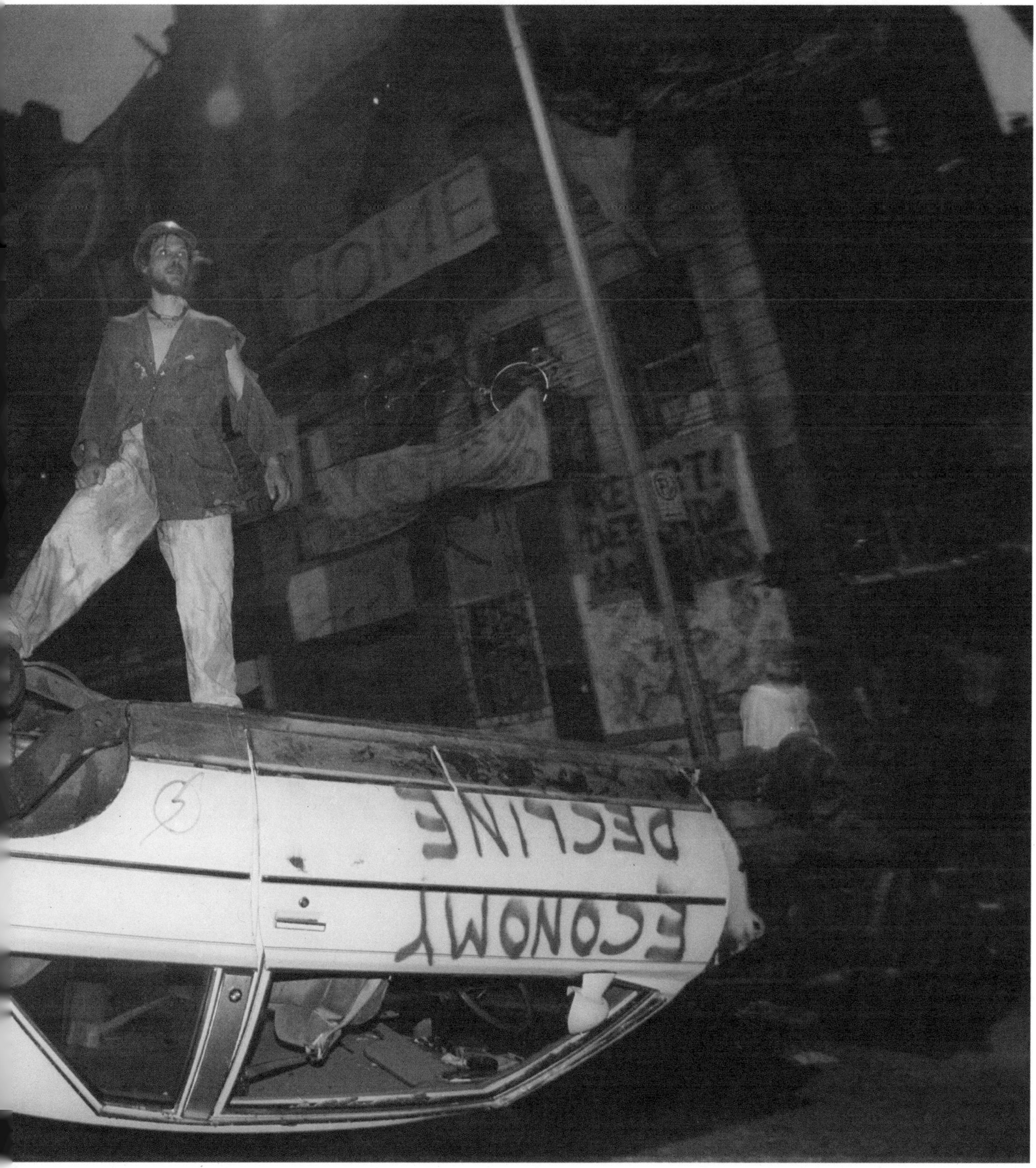

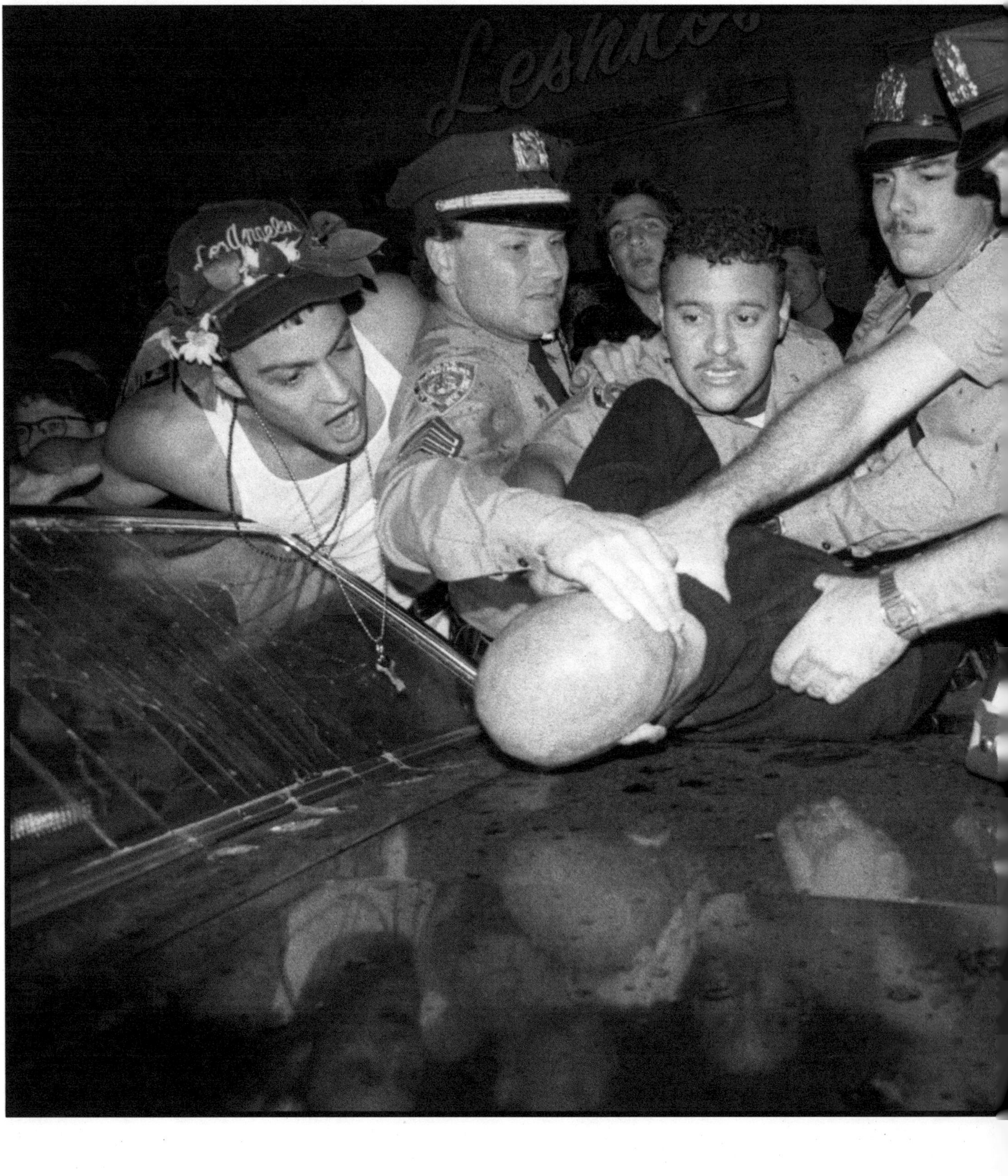
Leshko

TRACEY LITT

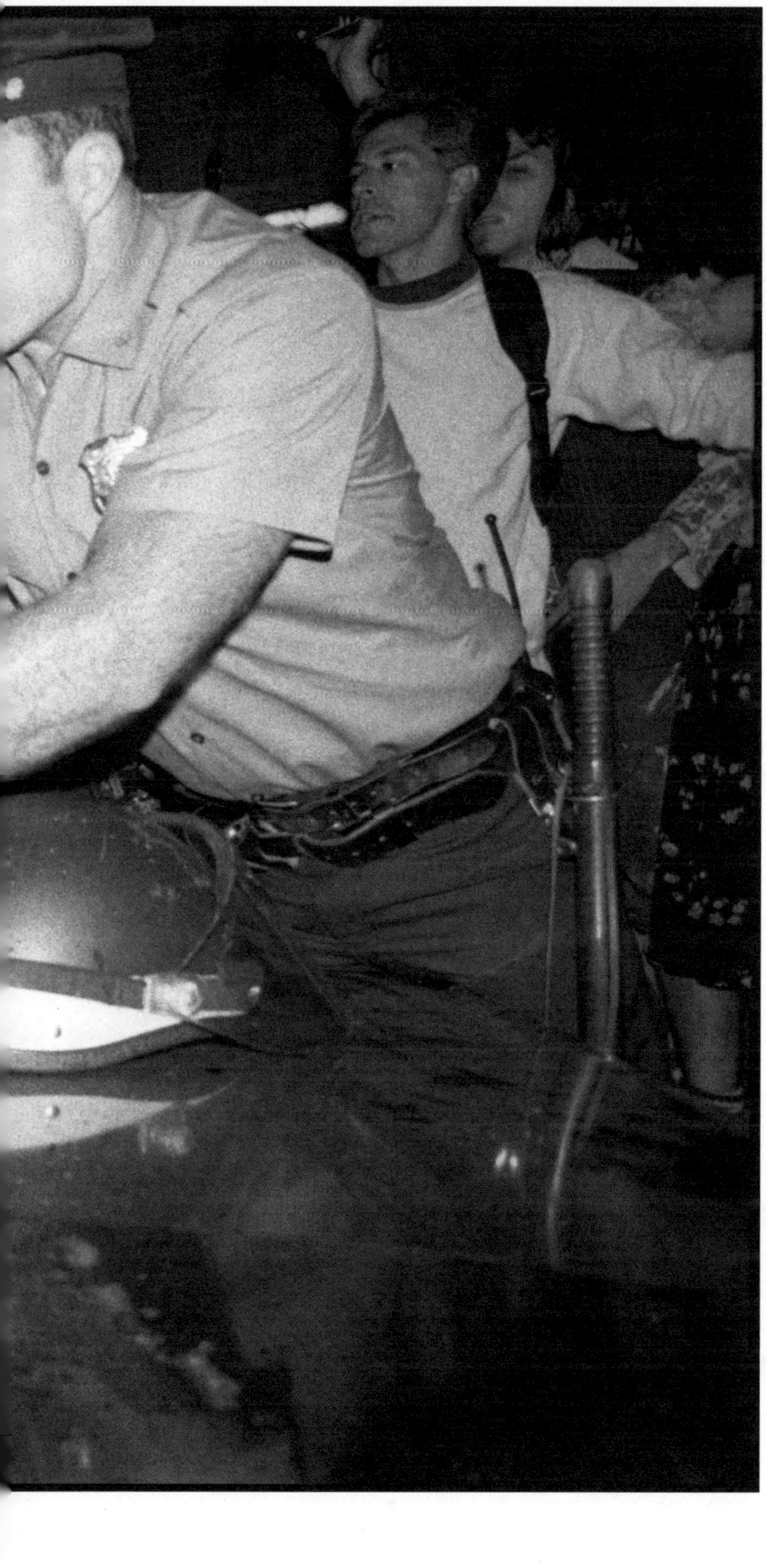

Manhattan, 1989. At Wigstock, an annual drag festival in Tompkins Square Park, police arrest a "skinhead" after he threw a bottle at a group of attendees.

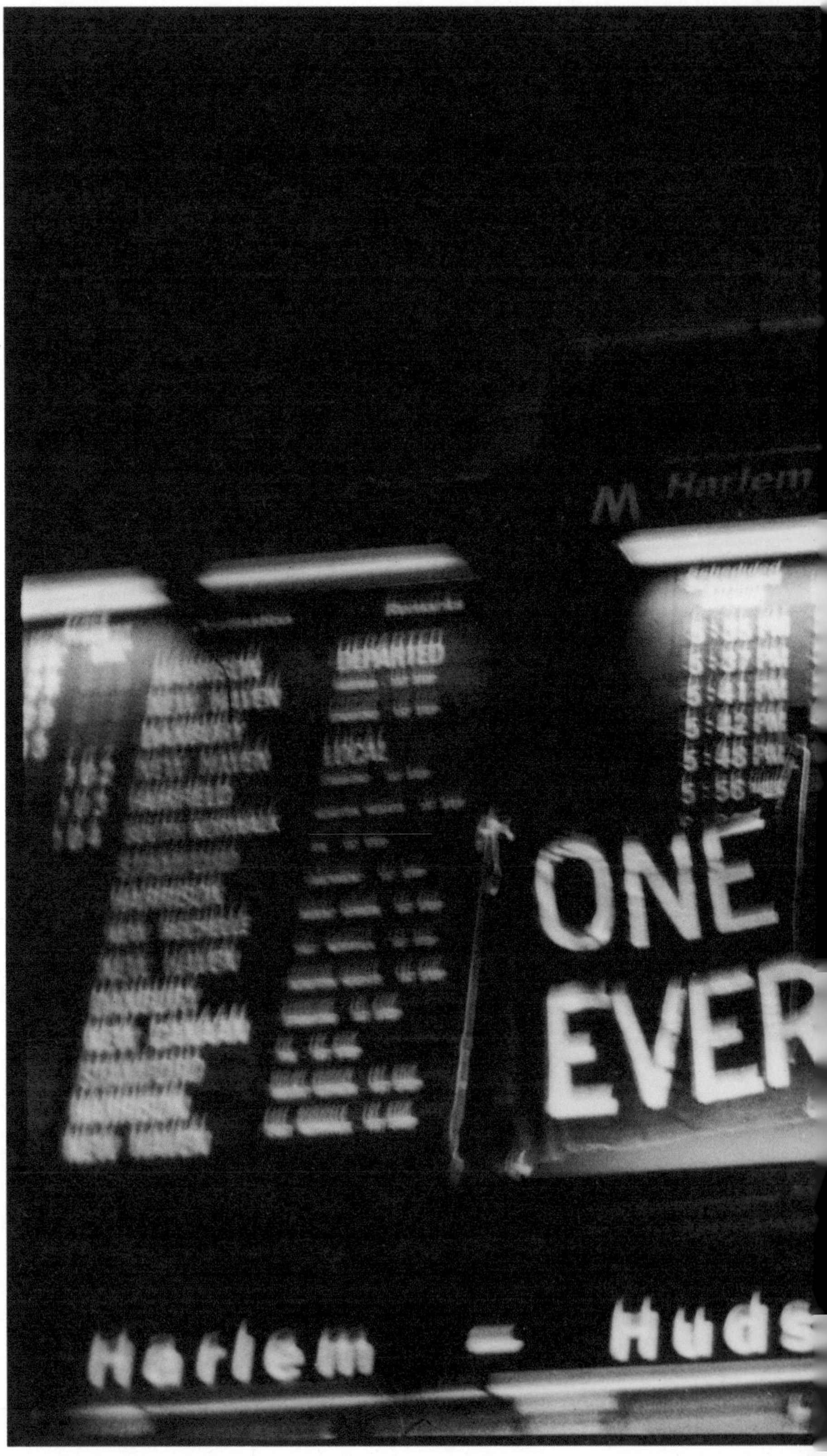

Manhattan, January 23, 1991. ACT UP "Day of Desperation" protest at Grand Central Station. The protest was staged in response to President George H. W. Bush spending billions of dollars on the Gulf War while claiming there was no money for much-needed increases in AIDS programs. On January 23rd ACT UP staged actions throughout the five boroughs, culminating in a large action at Grand Central.

DONA ANN MCADAMS

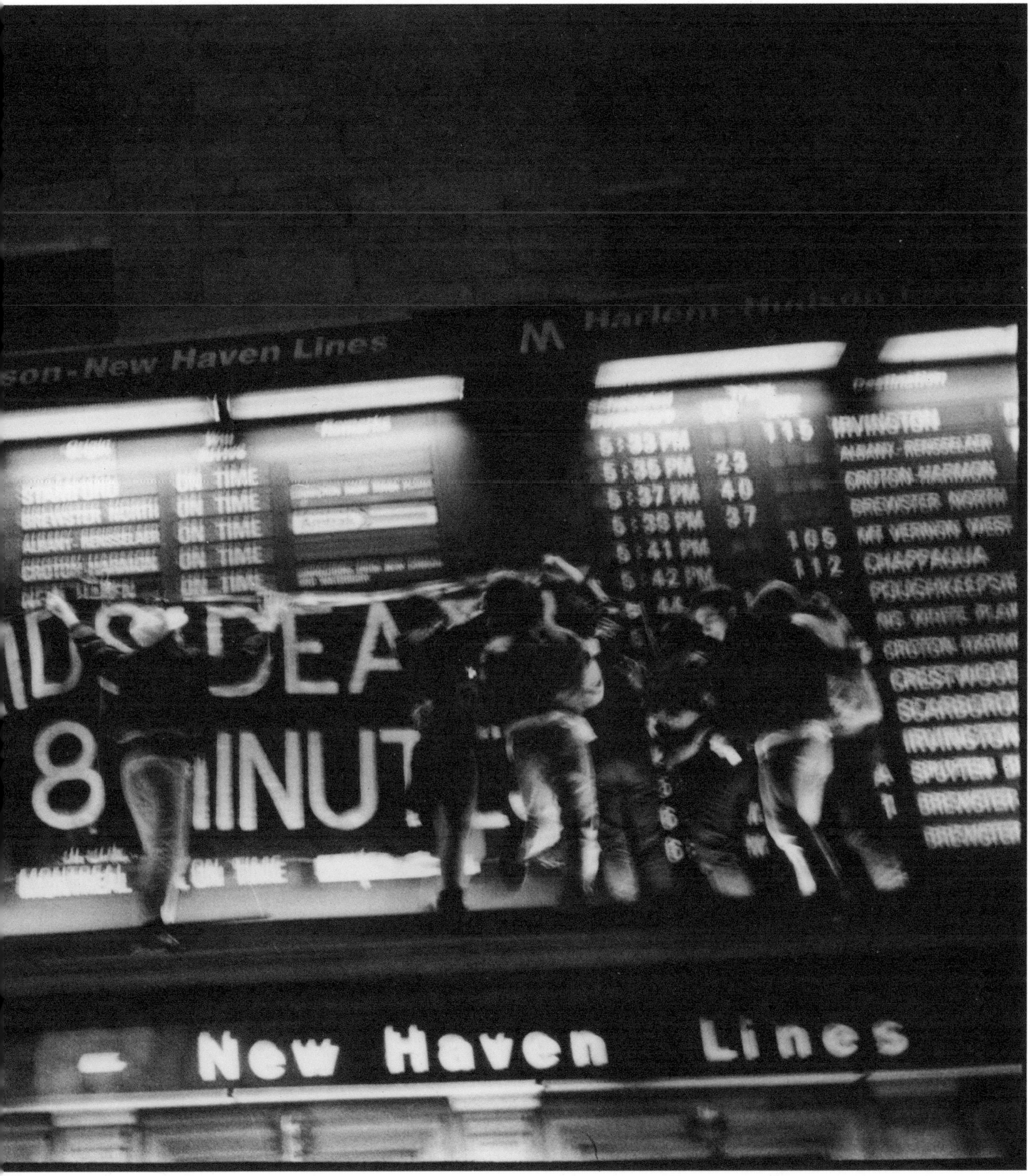

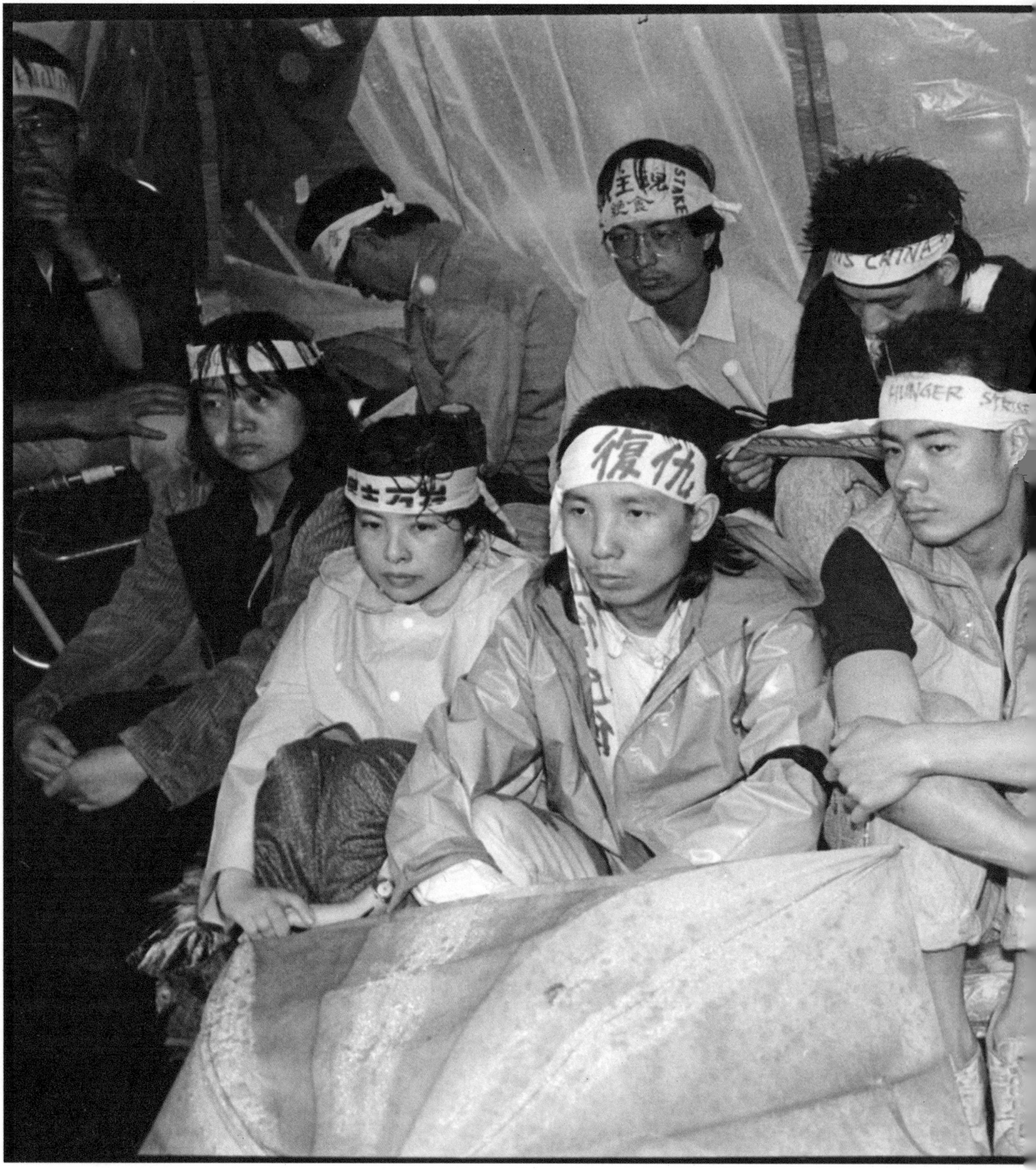
復仇
HUNGER

THOMAS MCGOVERN

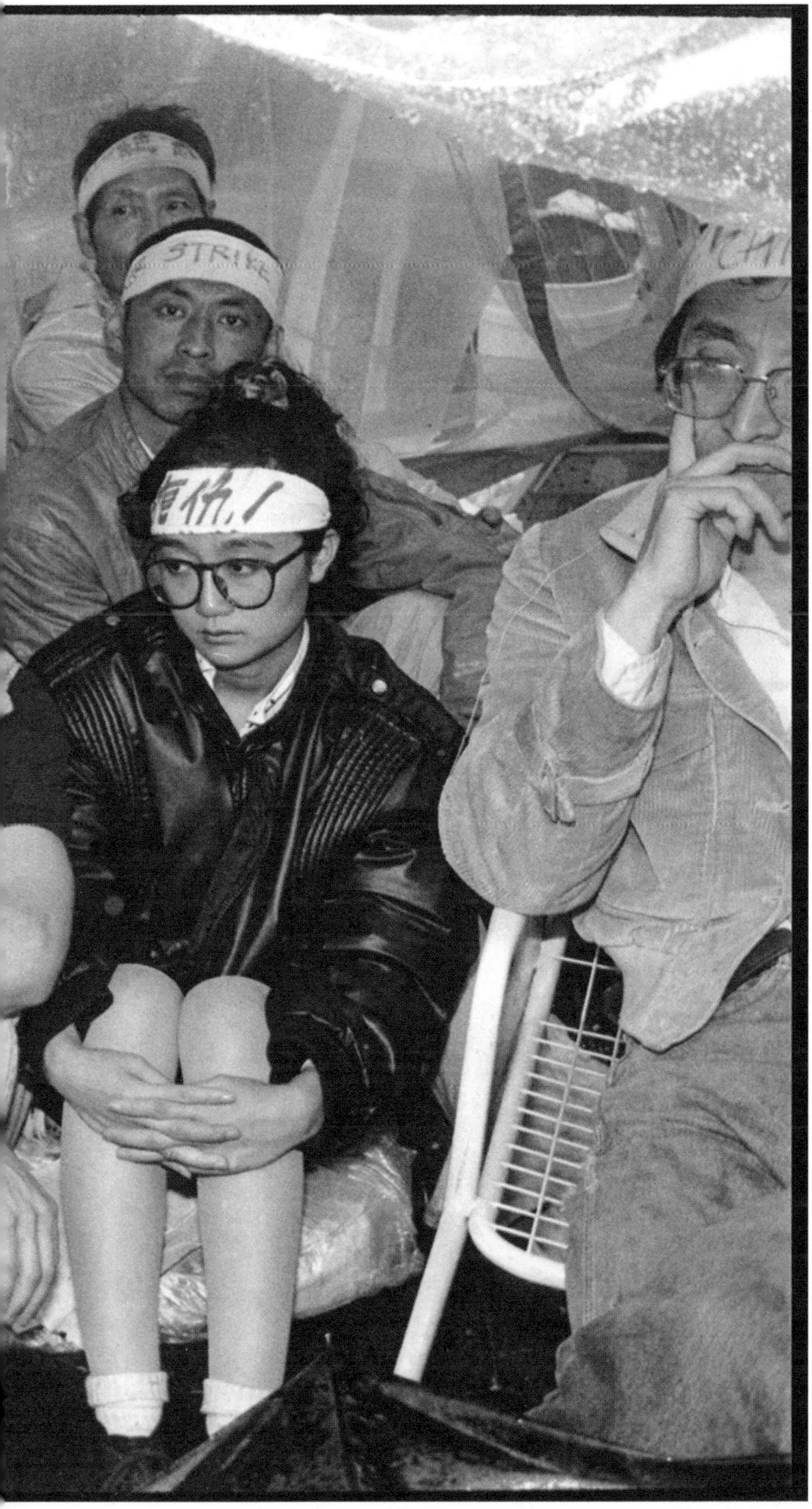

Manhattan, 1989. New Yorkers at a Chinese pro-democracy demonstration not long after the Tiananmen Square massacre.

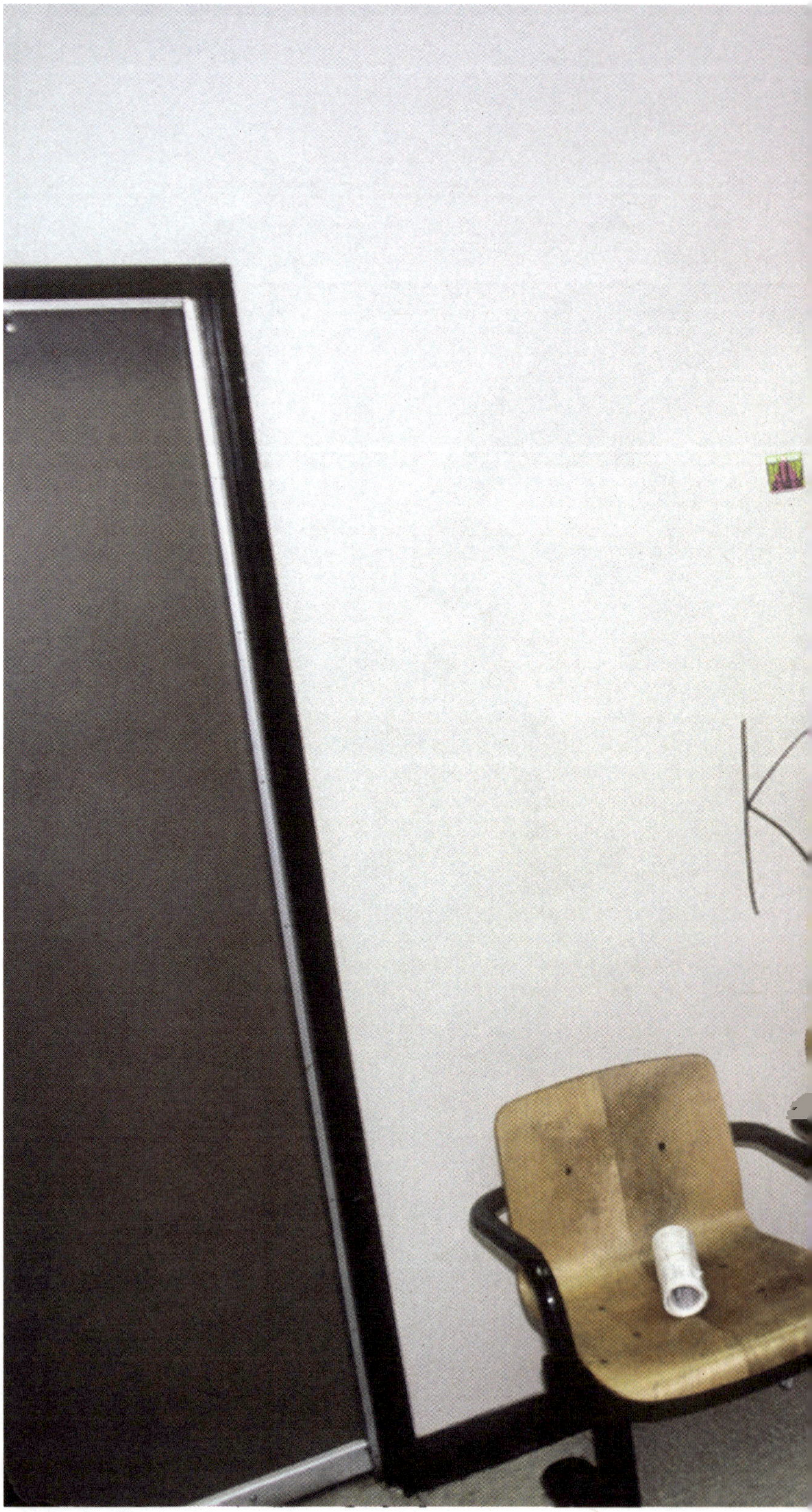

Manhattan, 1989. ACT UP civil disobedience at St. Vincent's Hospital.

TOMAS MUSCIONICO

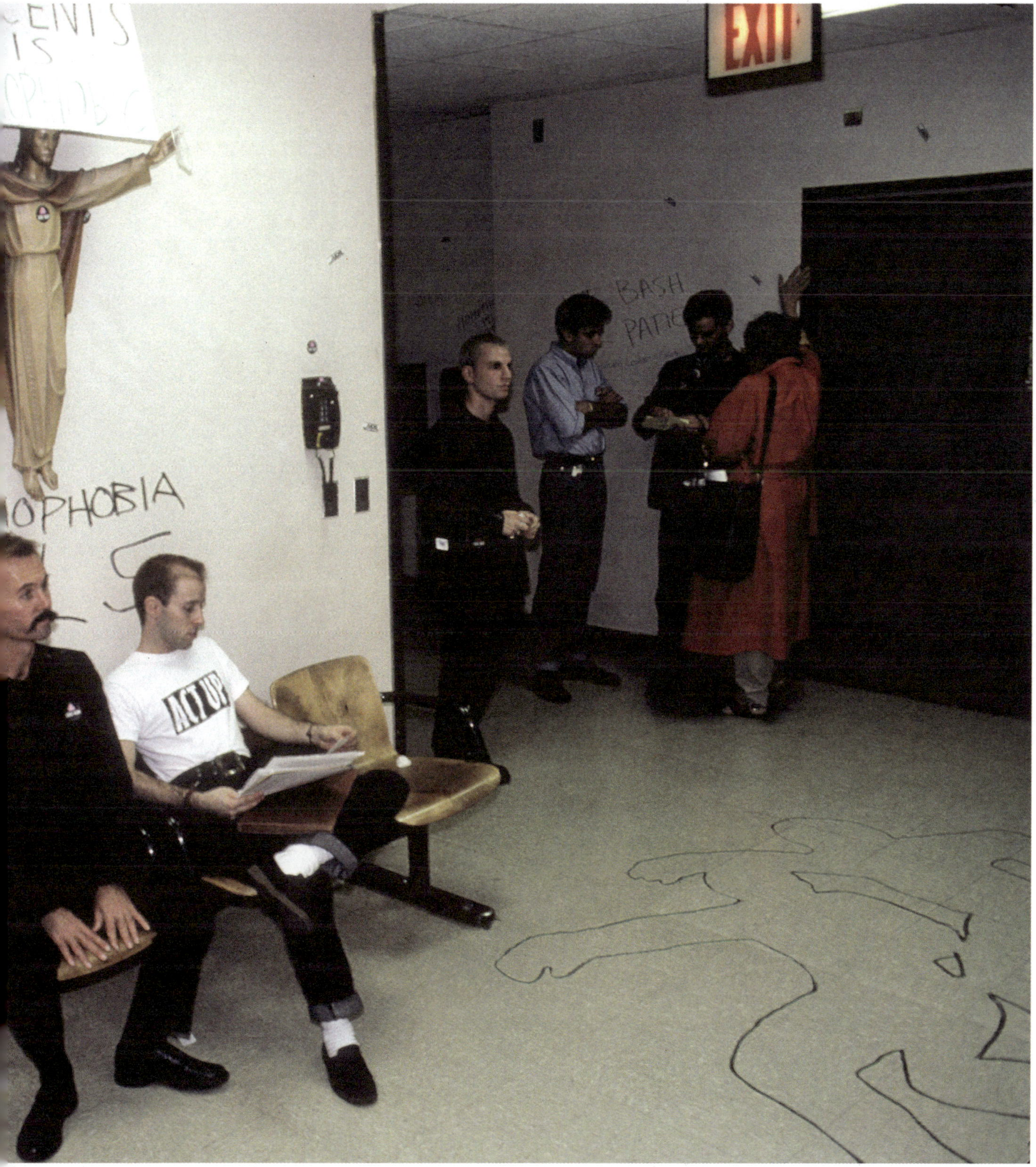

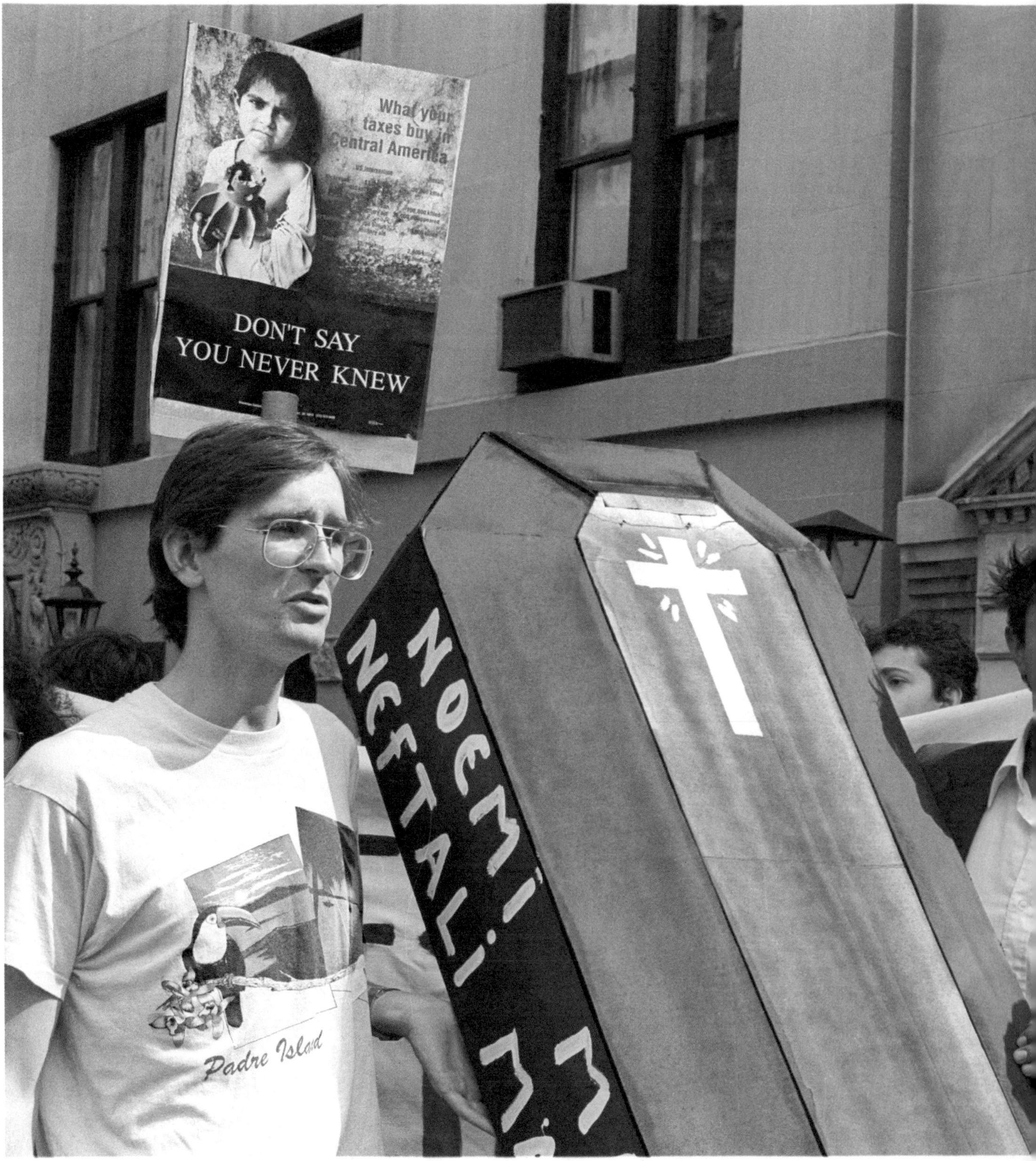
What your taxes buy in Central America
DON'T SAY
YOU NEVER KNEW
NOEMI M
NEFTALI M
Padre Island

EDWIN PAGÁN

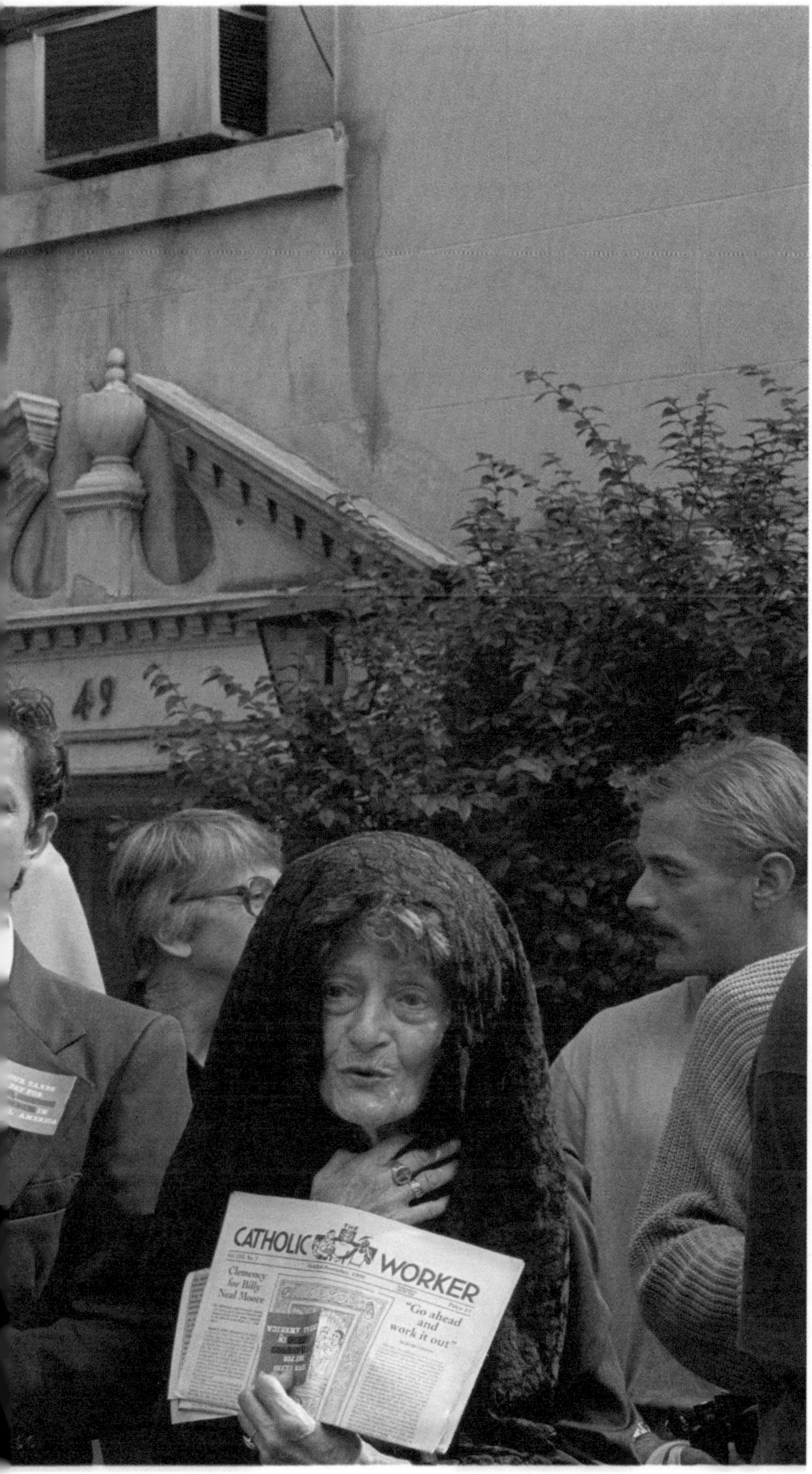

Manhattan, September 30, 1990. A group of Salvadoran activists and supporters make their way to the United Nations during the World Summit for Children. The protest was called to bring attention to murders by Salvadoran death squads despite a UN-brokered agreement between the government and Frente Farabundo Martí para la Liberación Nacional (FMLN). The escalation in fighting was preceded by the murder of six Jesuit priests the previous year.

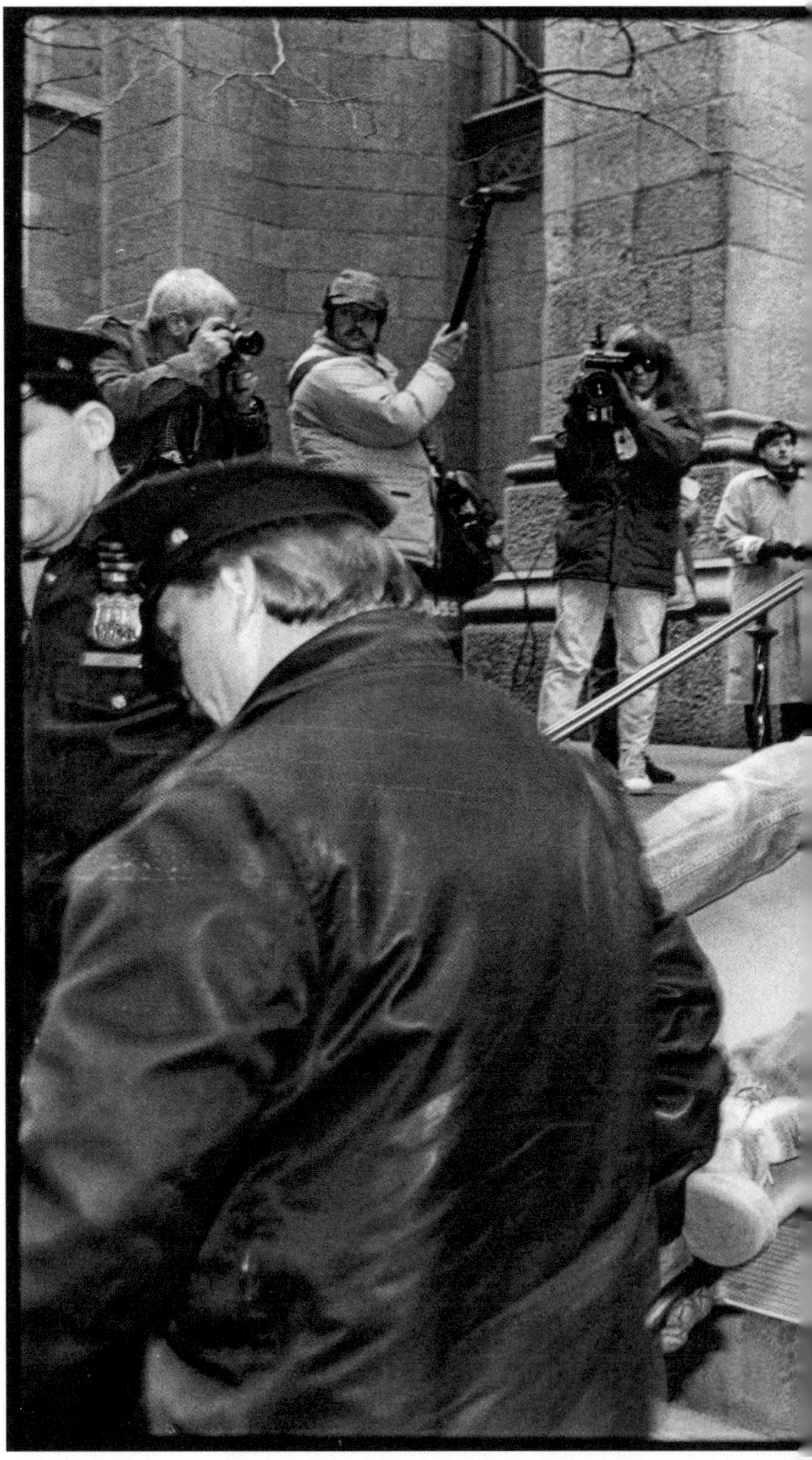

Manhattan, December 10, 1989.
A handcuffed ACT UP protester is removed from St. Patrick's Cathedral during the Stop the Church direct action.

BRIAN PALMER

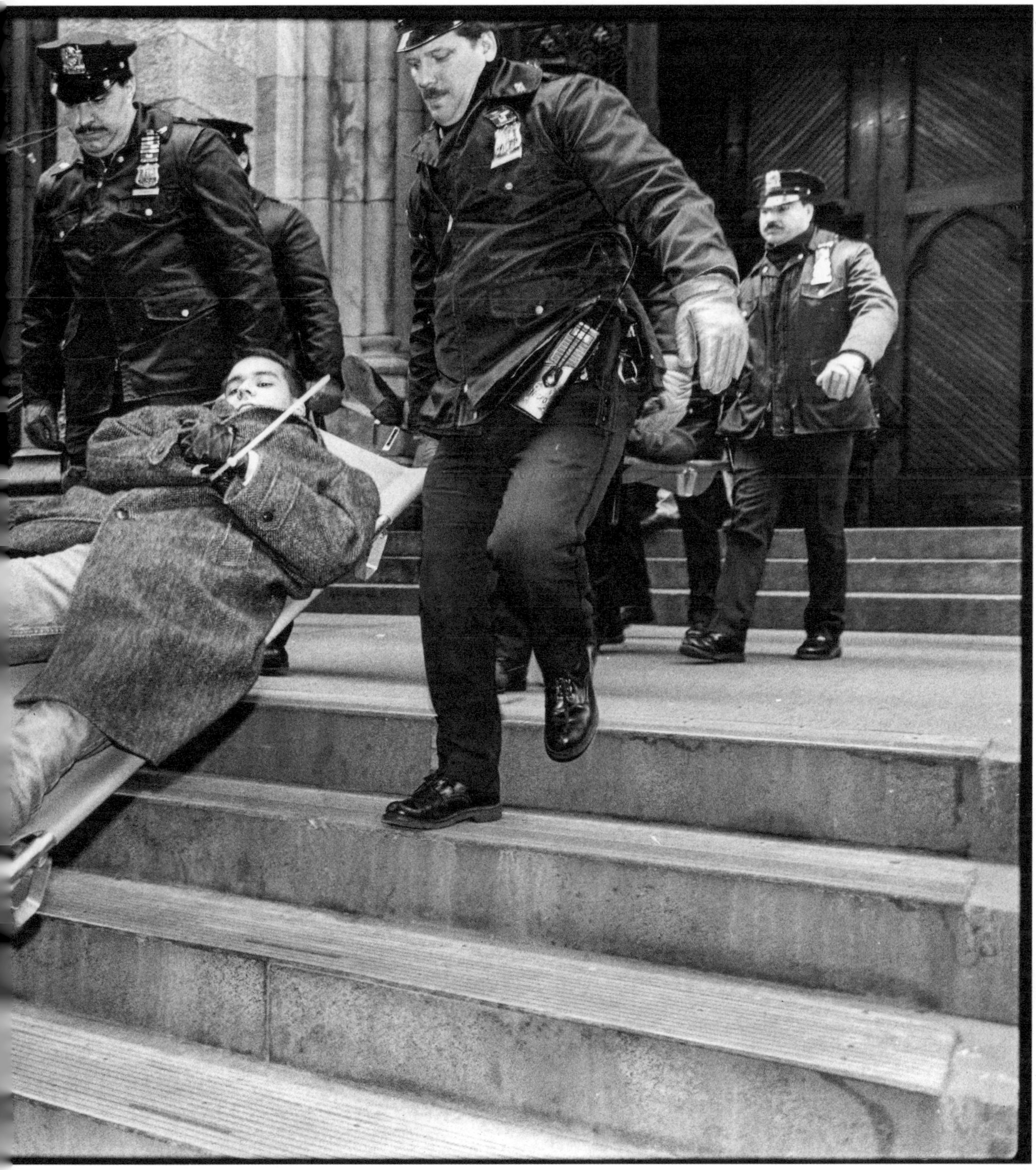

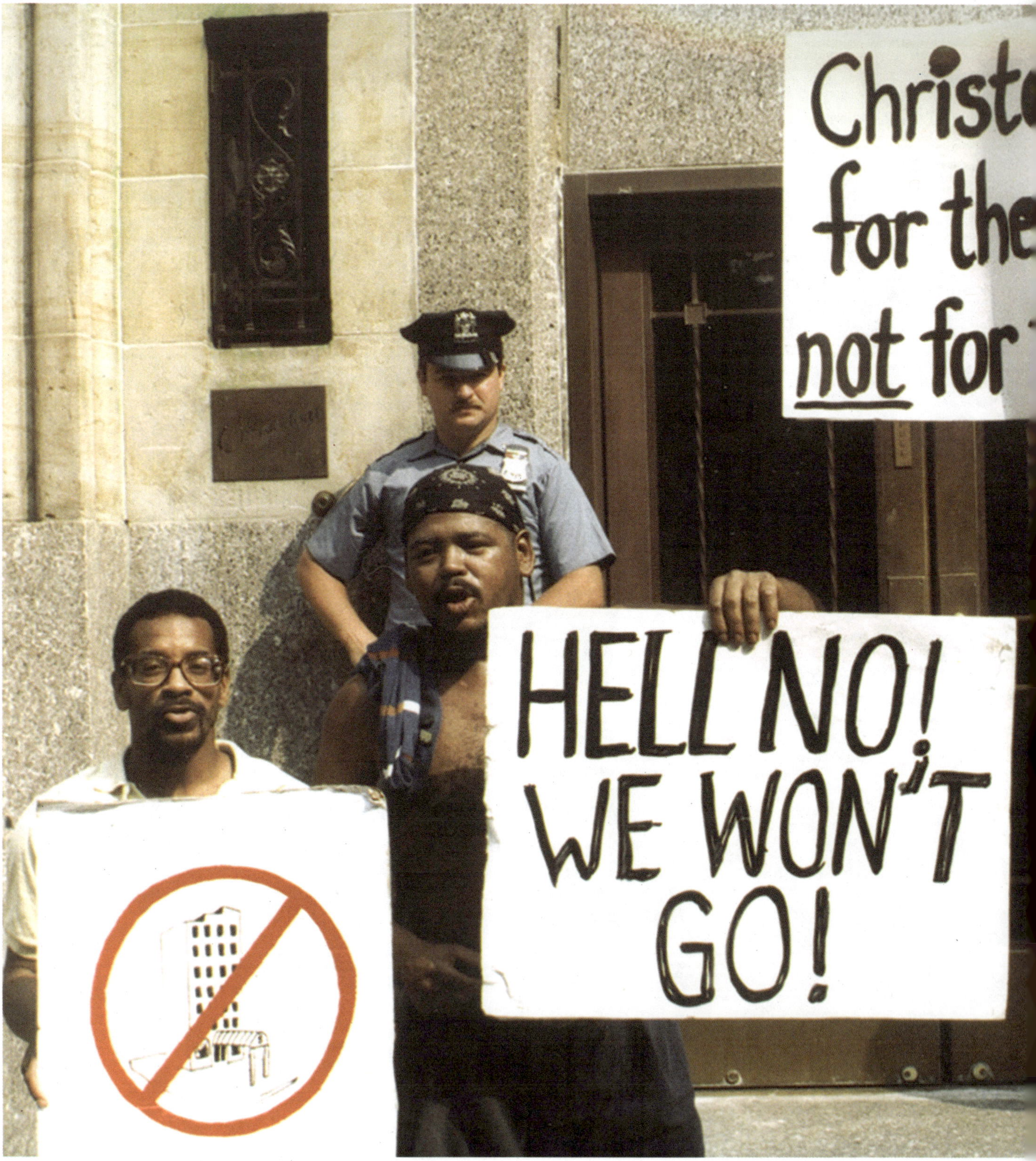
Christ
for the
not for
HELL NO!
WE WON'T
GO!

CLAYTON PATTERSON

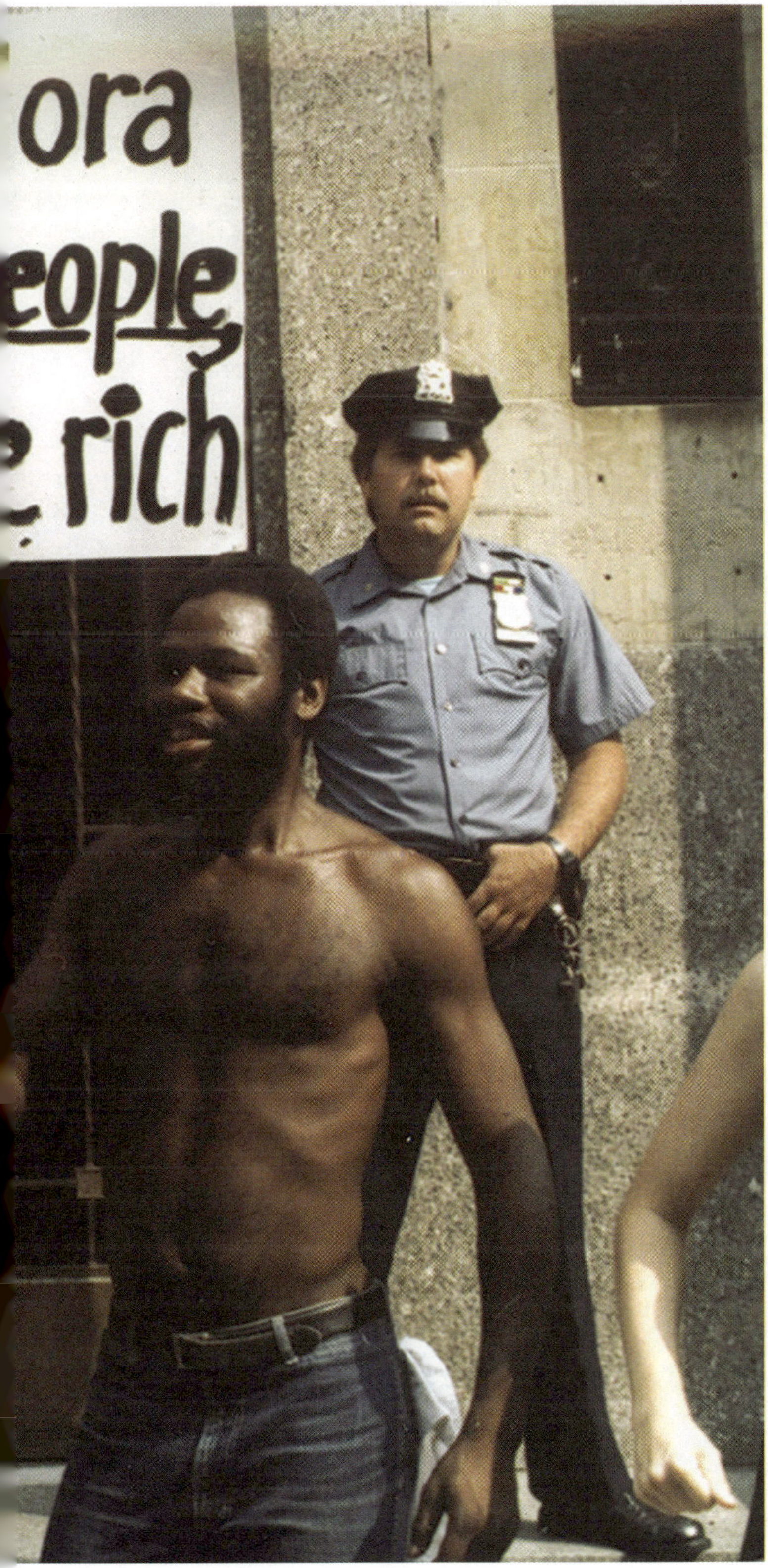

Manhattan, 1988. Protesters outside the Christodora in the East Village. The building was originally a settlement house for low-income and immigrant residents but was converted into a luxury condominium in 1986, becoming a symbol of inequality in the neighborhood.

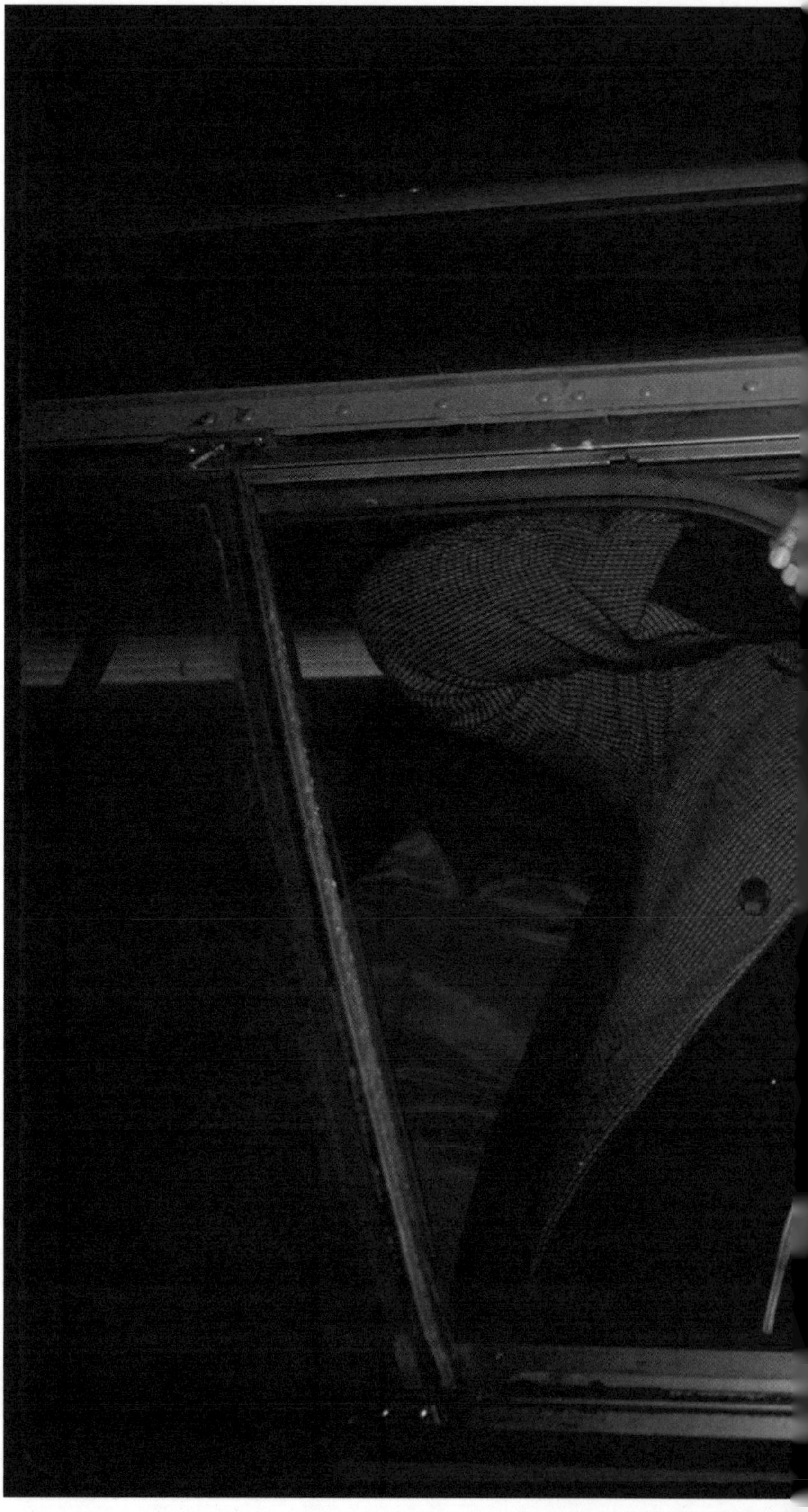

Brooklyn, 1989. Demonstrators are arrested at a civil rights march led by Rev. Al Sharpton during the 1990 trial of Keith Mondello. Mondello was tried for murder and manslaughter in the mob killing of African American youth Yusef Hawkins in Bensonhurst, Brooklyn on August 23, 1989.

MARK PETERSON

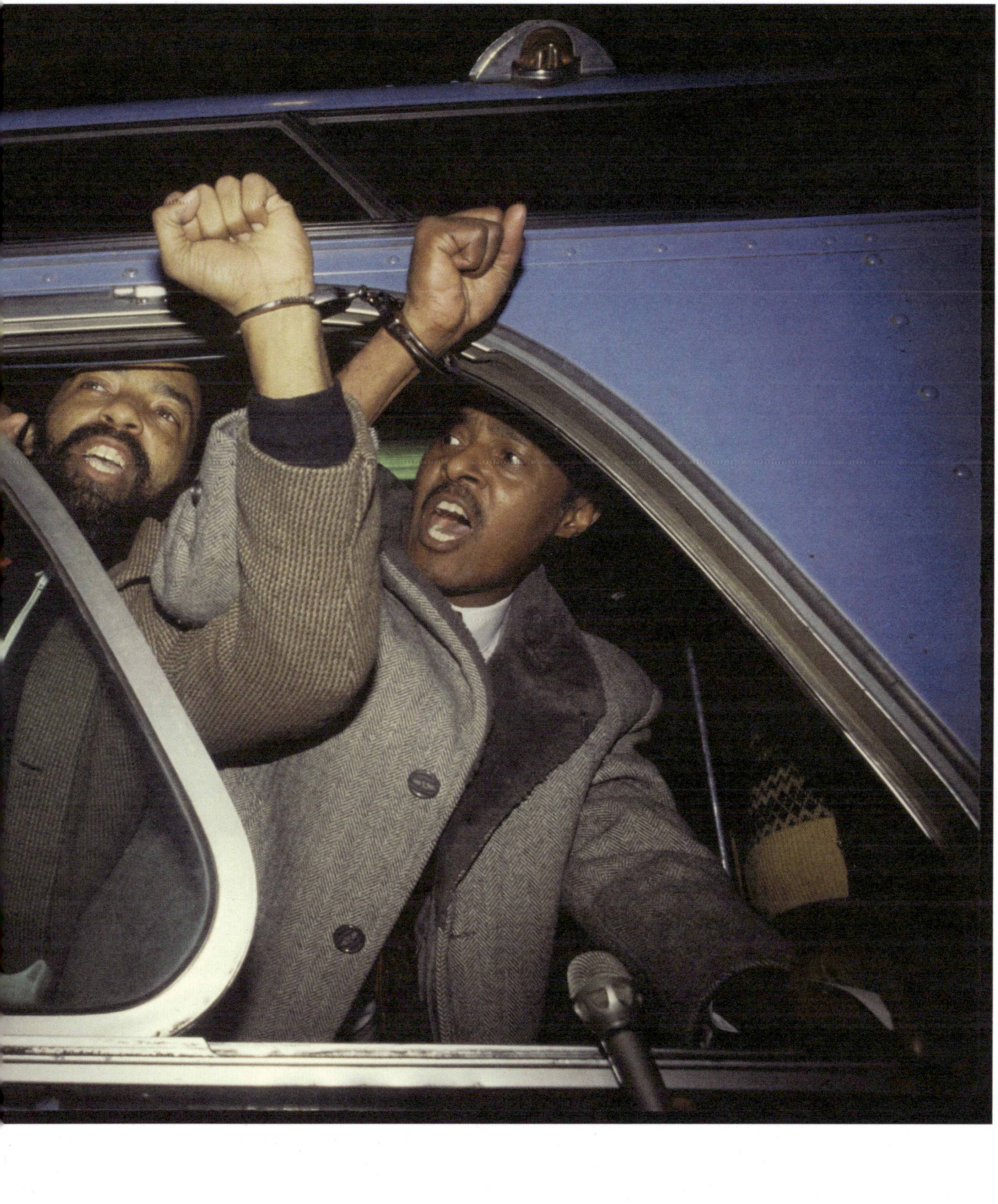

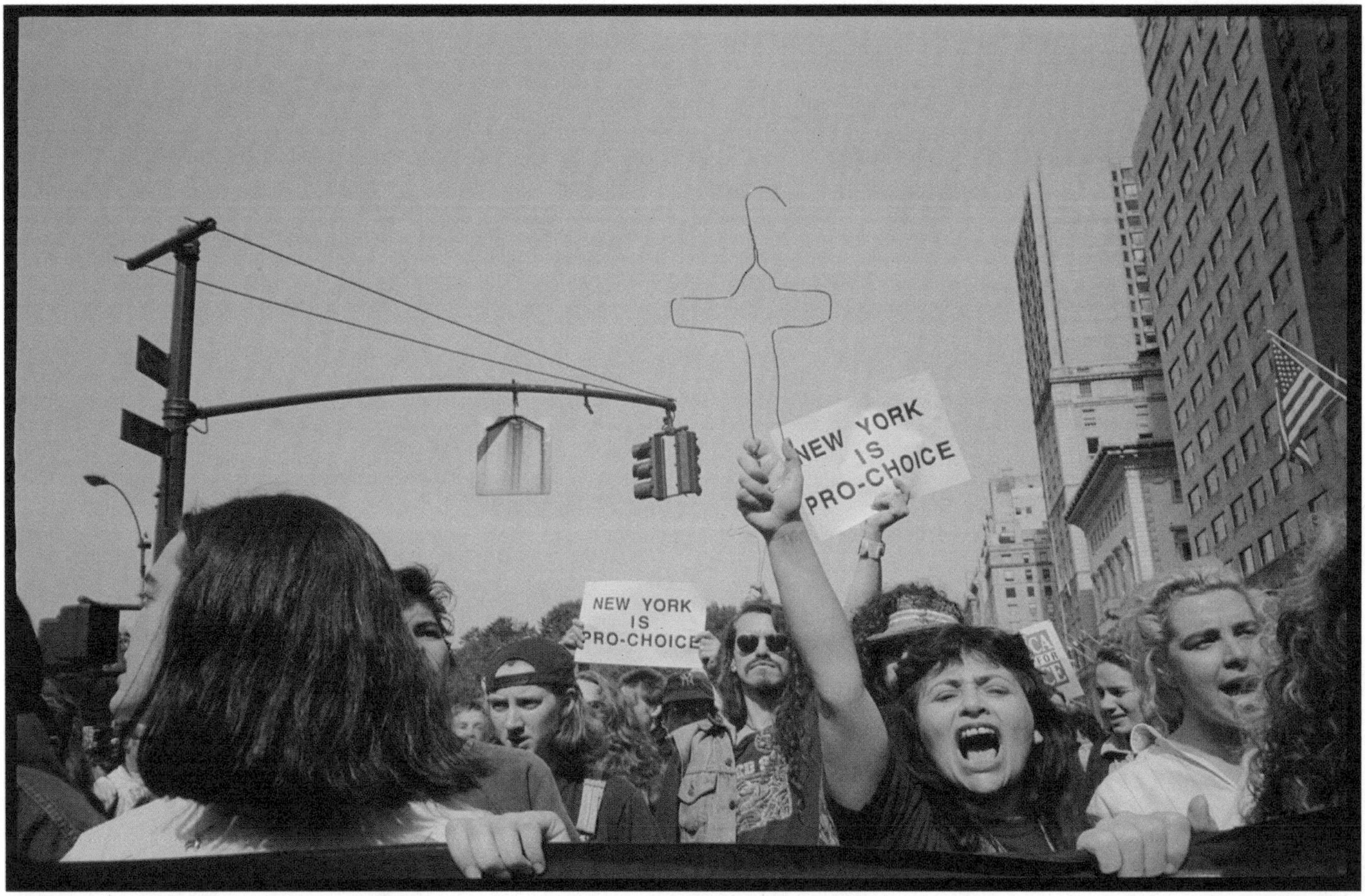

Manhattan, 1992. Pro-choice march.

SANDRA-LEE PHIPPS

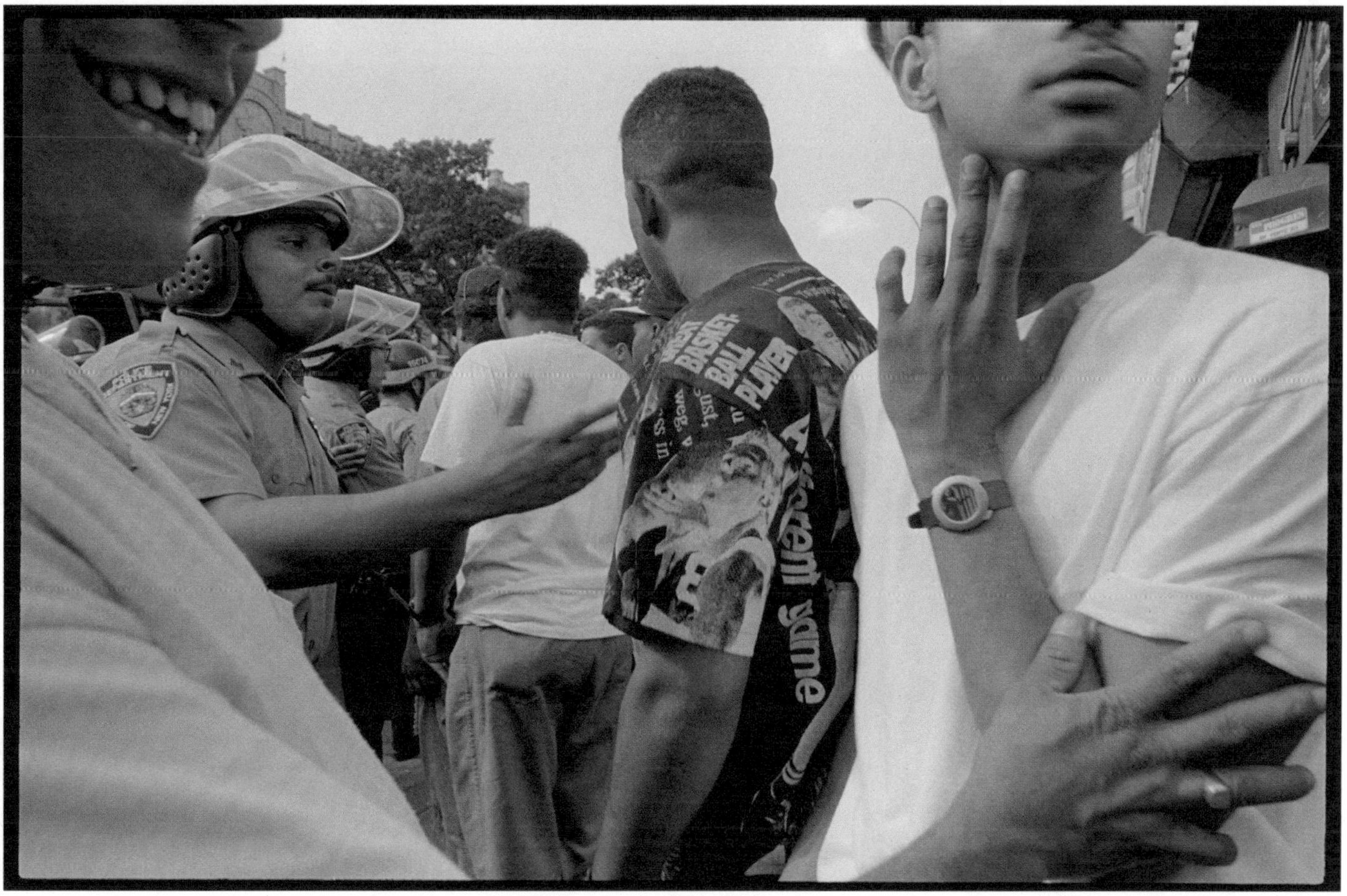

Manhattan, 1992. Crowds react to the police during the Washington Heights riots over the fatal police shooting of Jose "Kiko" Garcia, a Dominican immigrant. The riots covered a 40-square-block area of New York City and took place from July 4-7, 1992.

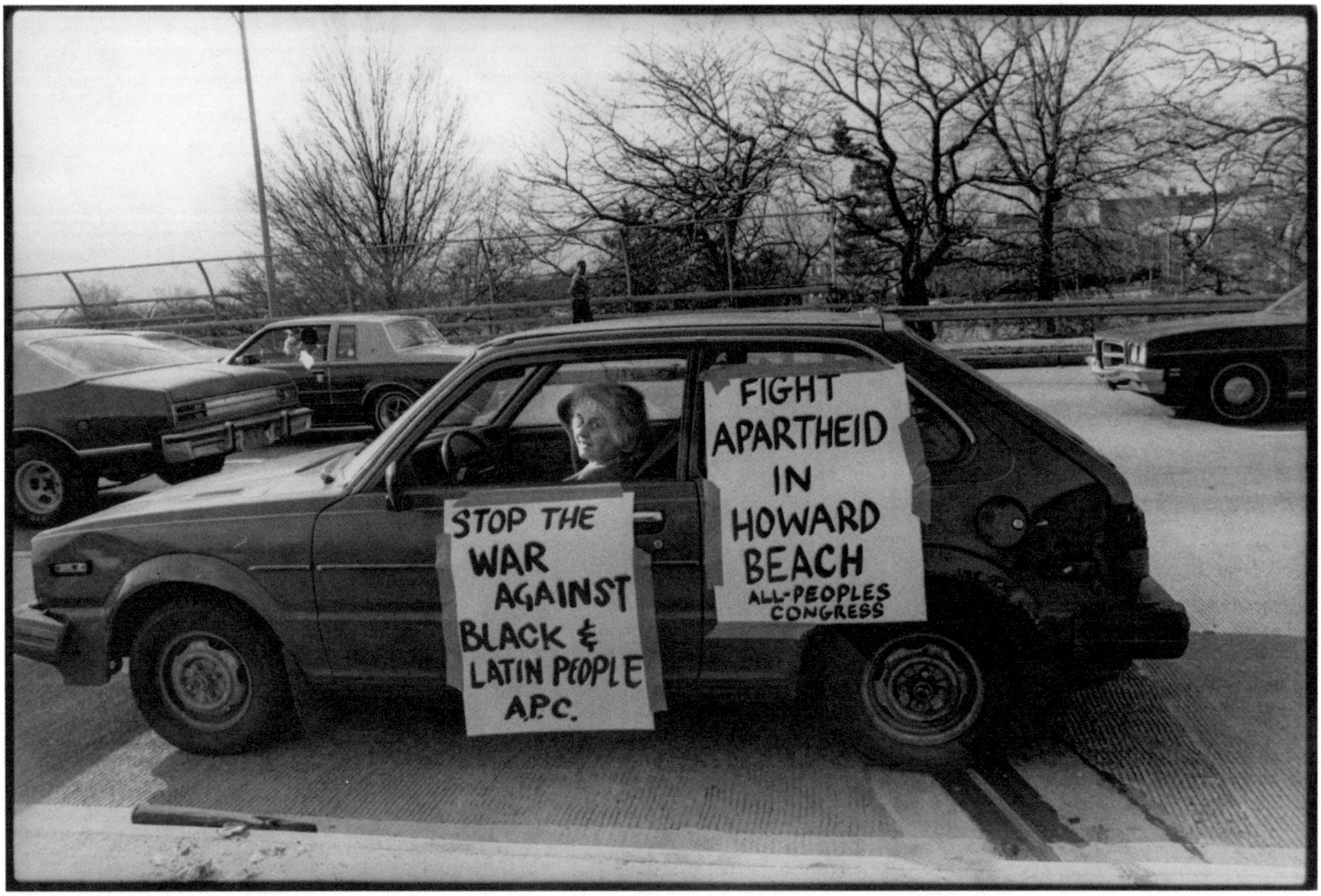

Queens, 1986. Protest in Howard Beach following the death of Michael Griffith, an African American man who was hit by a car while fleeing a white mob.

SYLVIA PLACHY

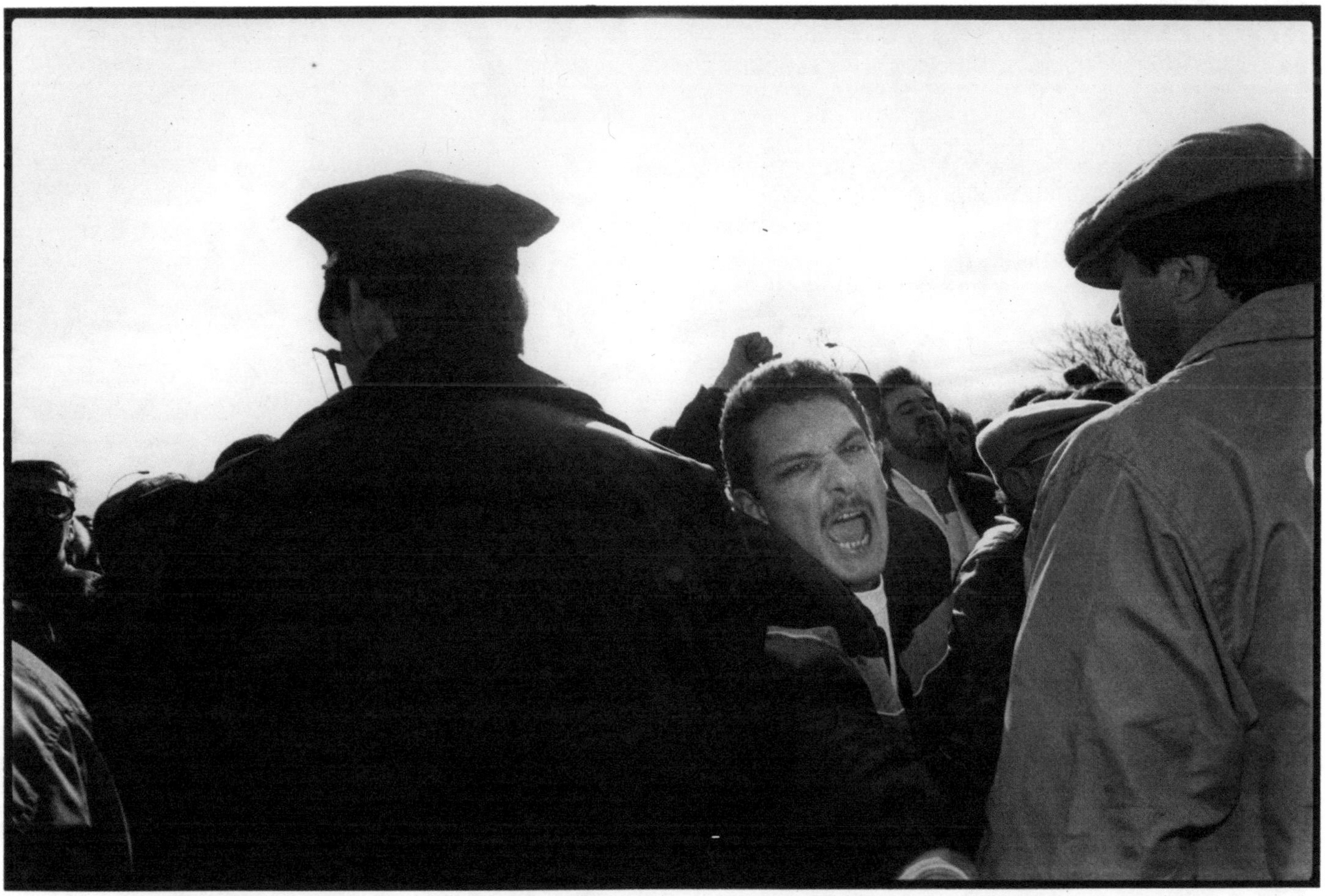

Queens, 1986, A counter-demonstrator protests a Rev. Al Sharpton led march in Howard Beach following the death of Michael Griffith, an African American man who was hit by a car while fleeing a white mob.

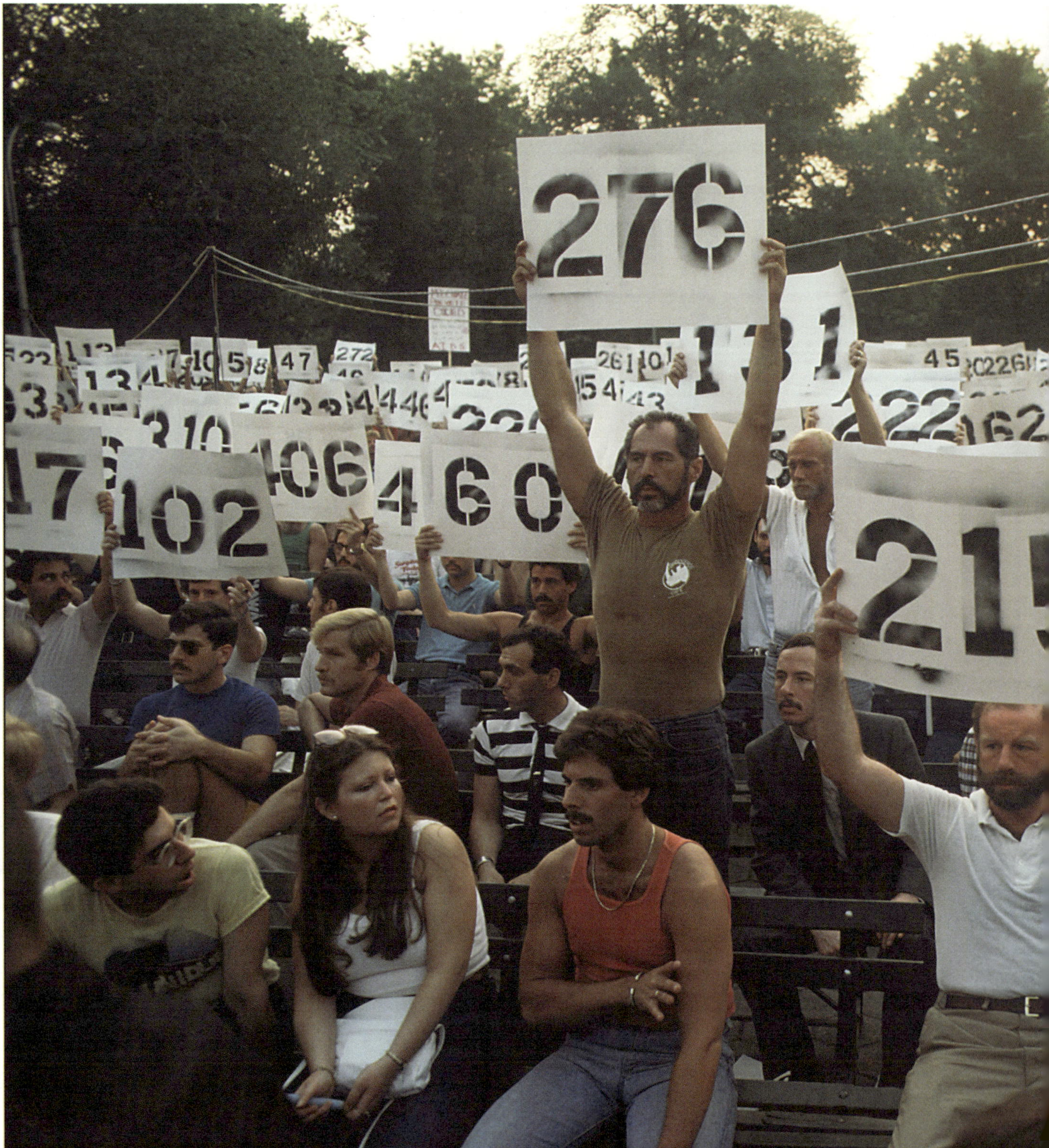
276
406
102
460
47

ALON REININGER

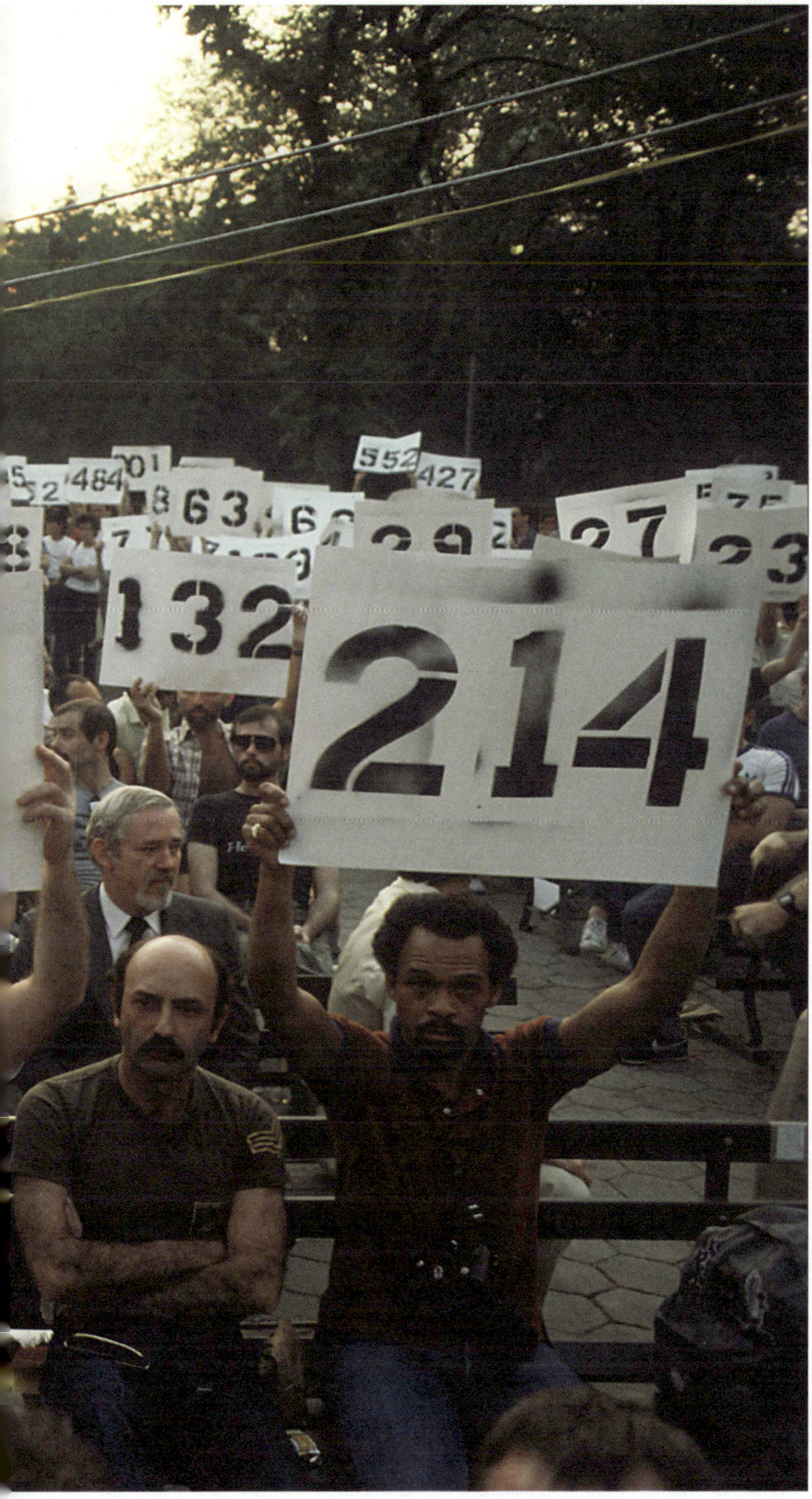

Manhattan, June 1983. Memorial to AIDS victims in Central Park.

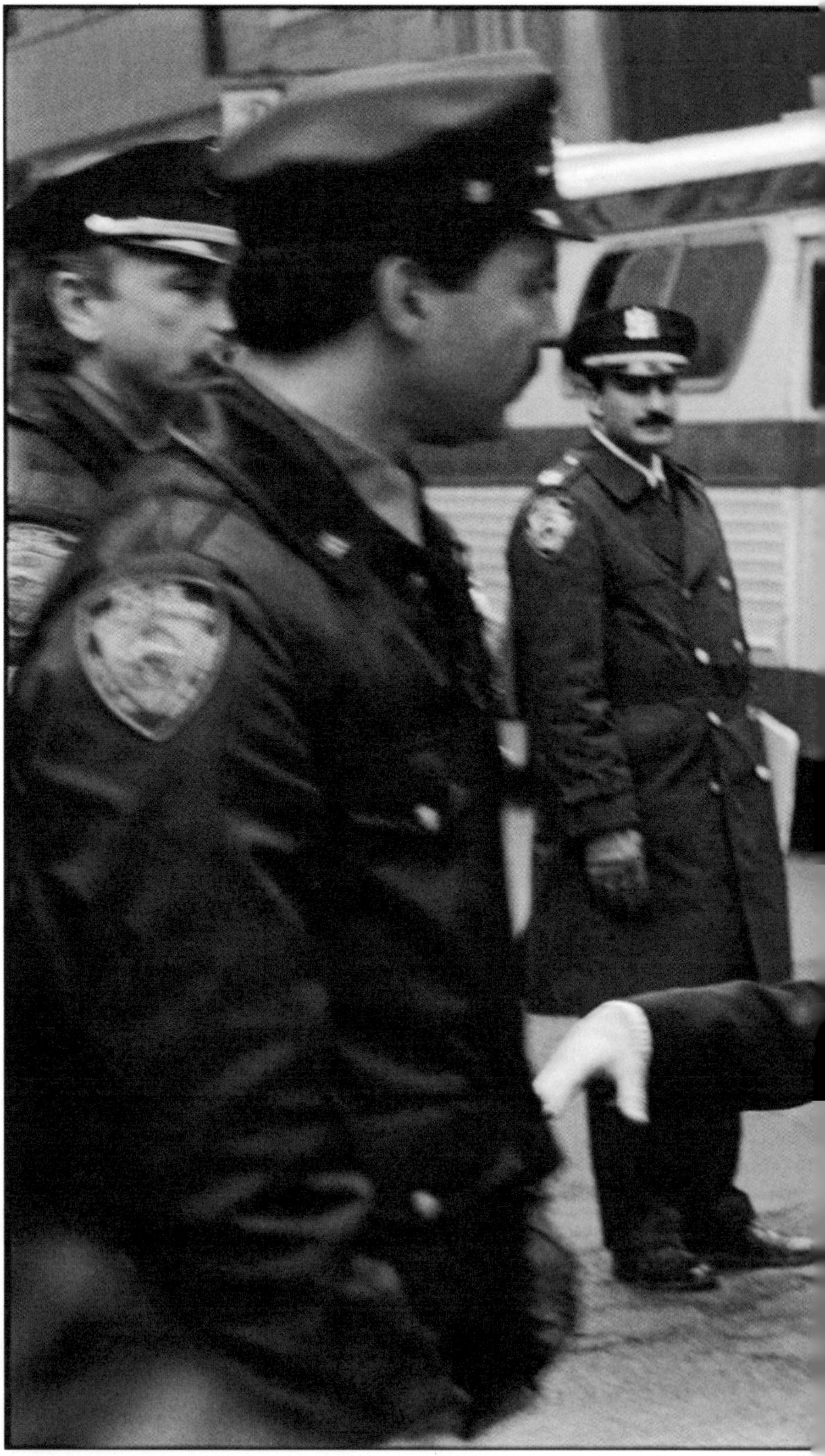

Manhattan, March 24, 1988. ACT UP member Mark Harrington is arrested during a large demonstration on Wall Street in which over 100 people were arrested.

RICHARD RENALDI

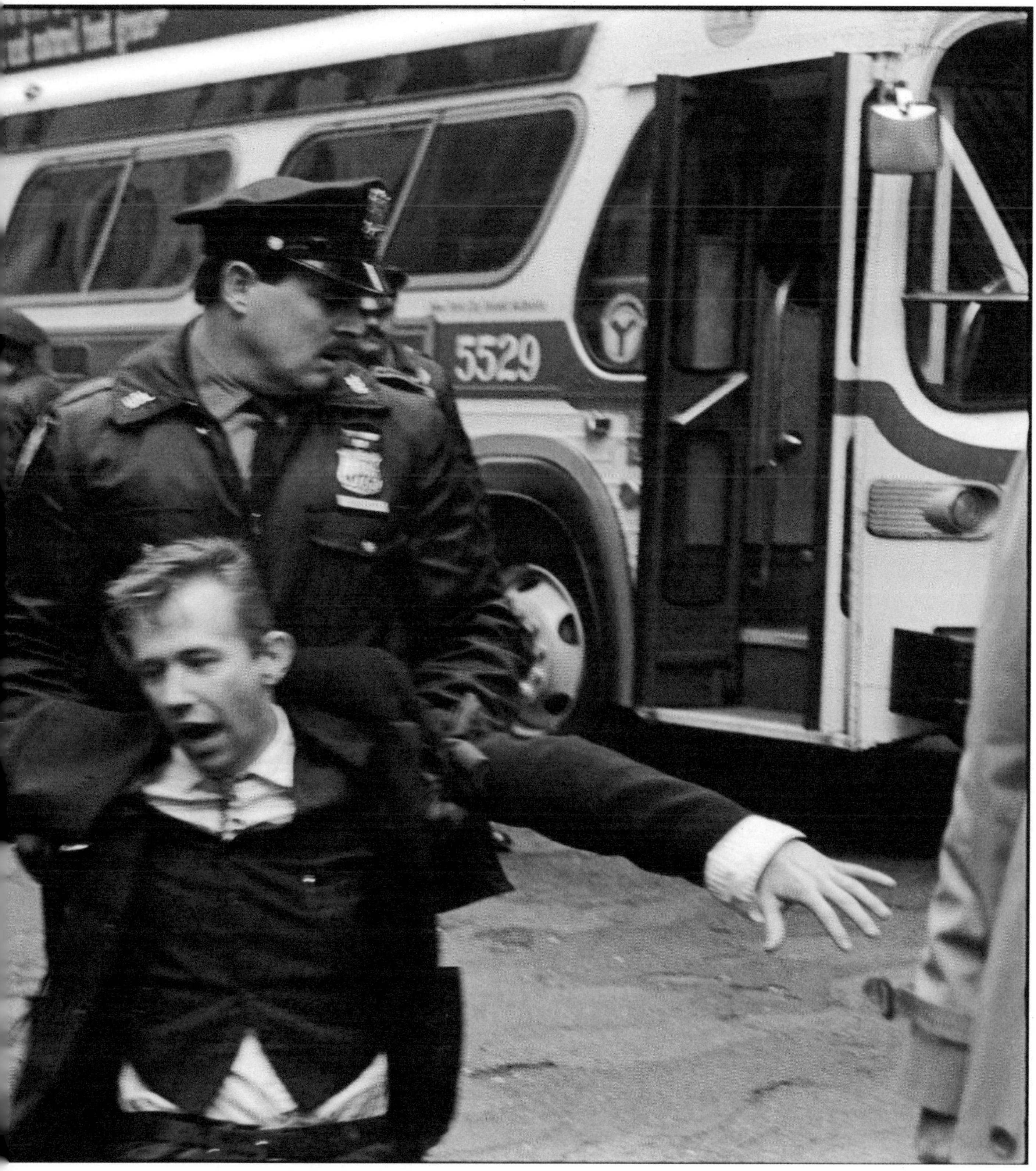

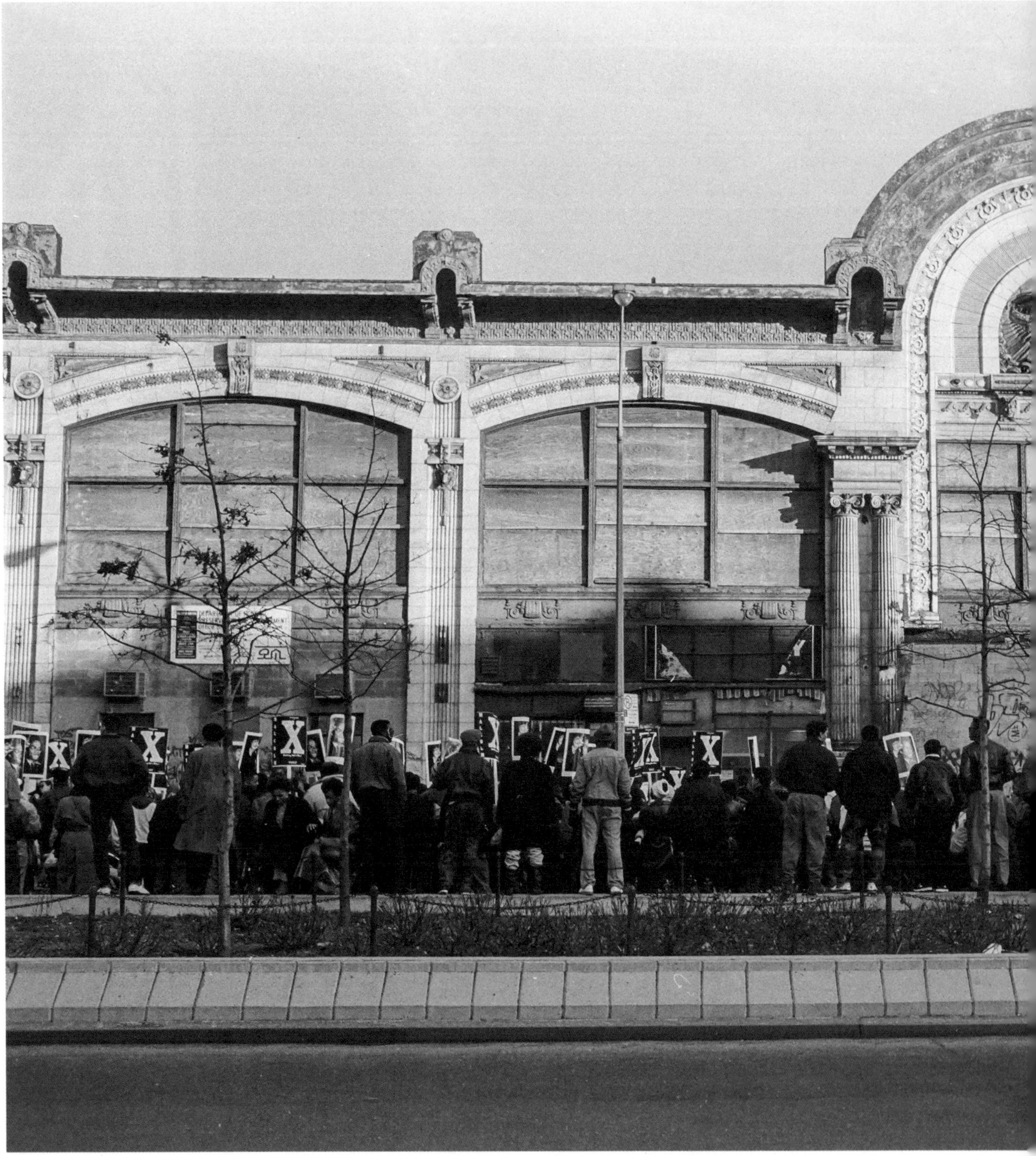
X

CLARENCE ELIE-RIVERA

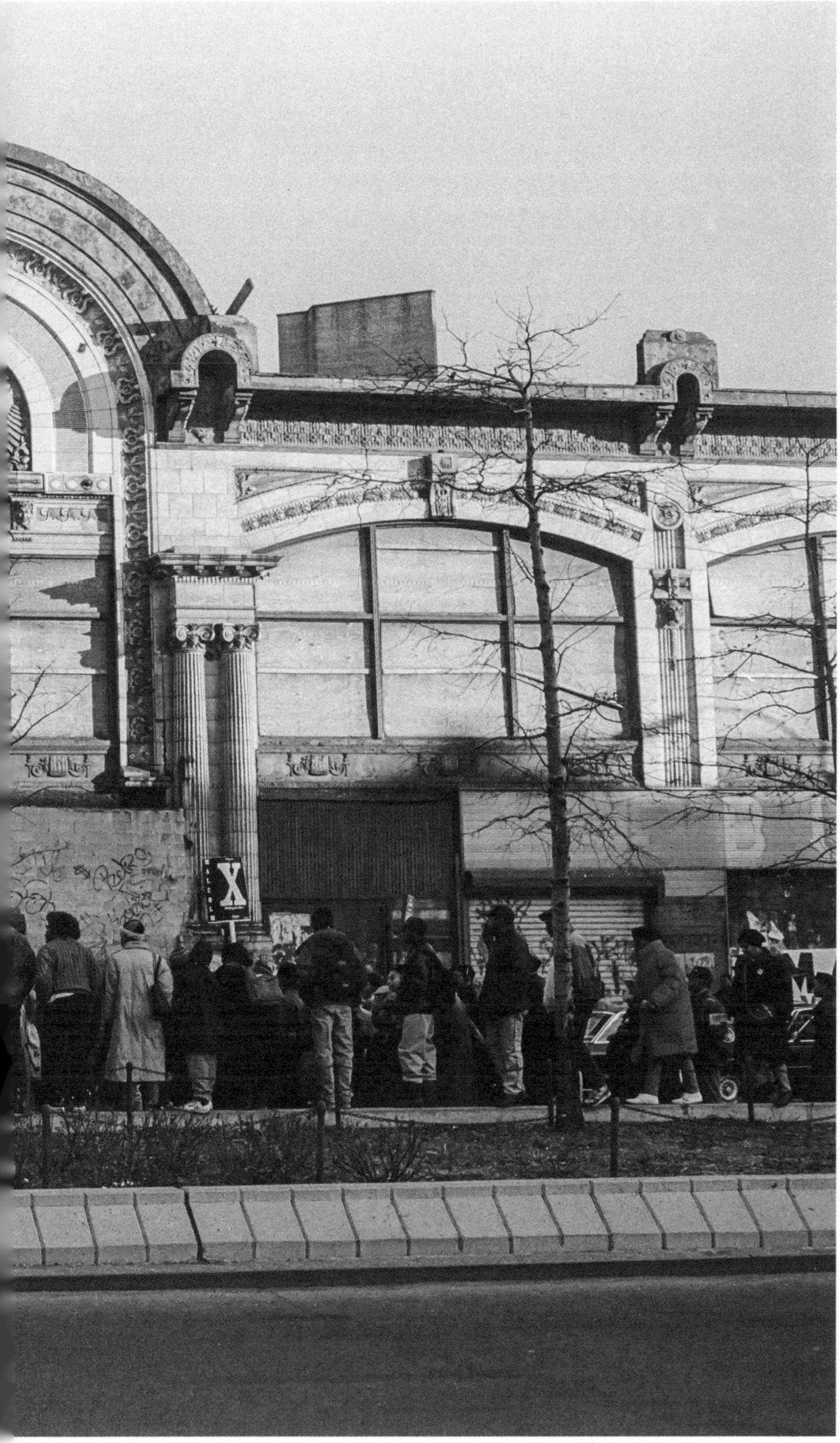

Manhattan, 1990. The December 12th Movement organized several protests, including this one outside the Audubon Ballroom in Harlem, against Columbia University's plan to demolish the Audubon Ballroom and replace it with a medical research facility. Malcolm X held meetings in the Ballroom and was assassinated there on February 21, 1965.The protests led to an agreement to preserve two thirds of the original facade and part of the interior ballroom was restored and made into a museum.

JOSEPH RODRIGUEZ

Manhattan, 1984. Children play at a Committee to Save East Harlem demonstration.

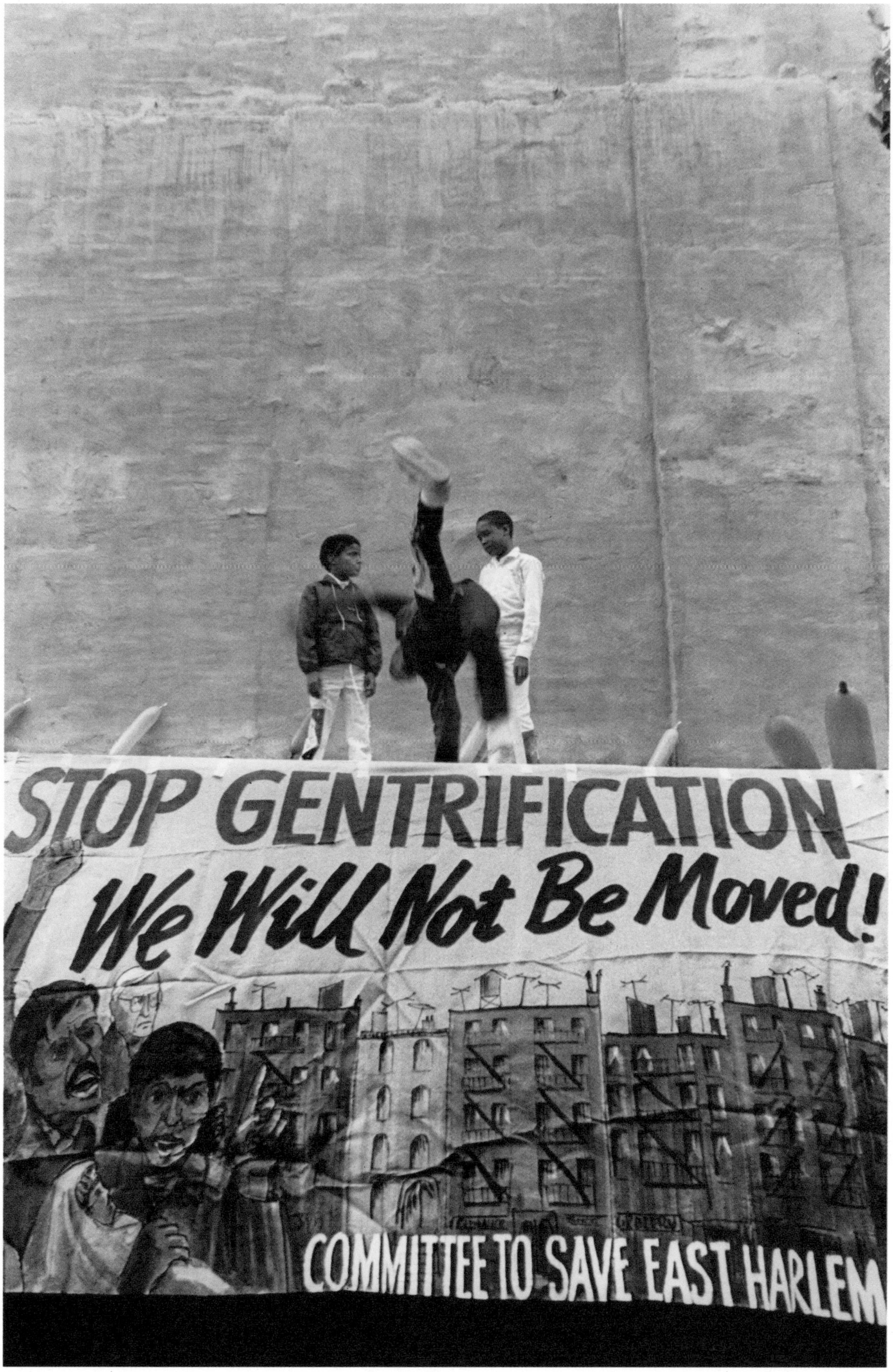
STOP GENTRIFICATION
We Will Not Be Moved!
COMMITTEE TO SAVE EAST HARLEM

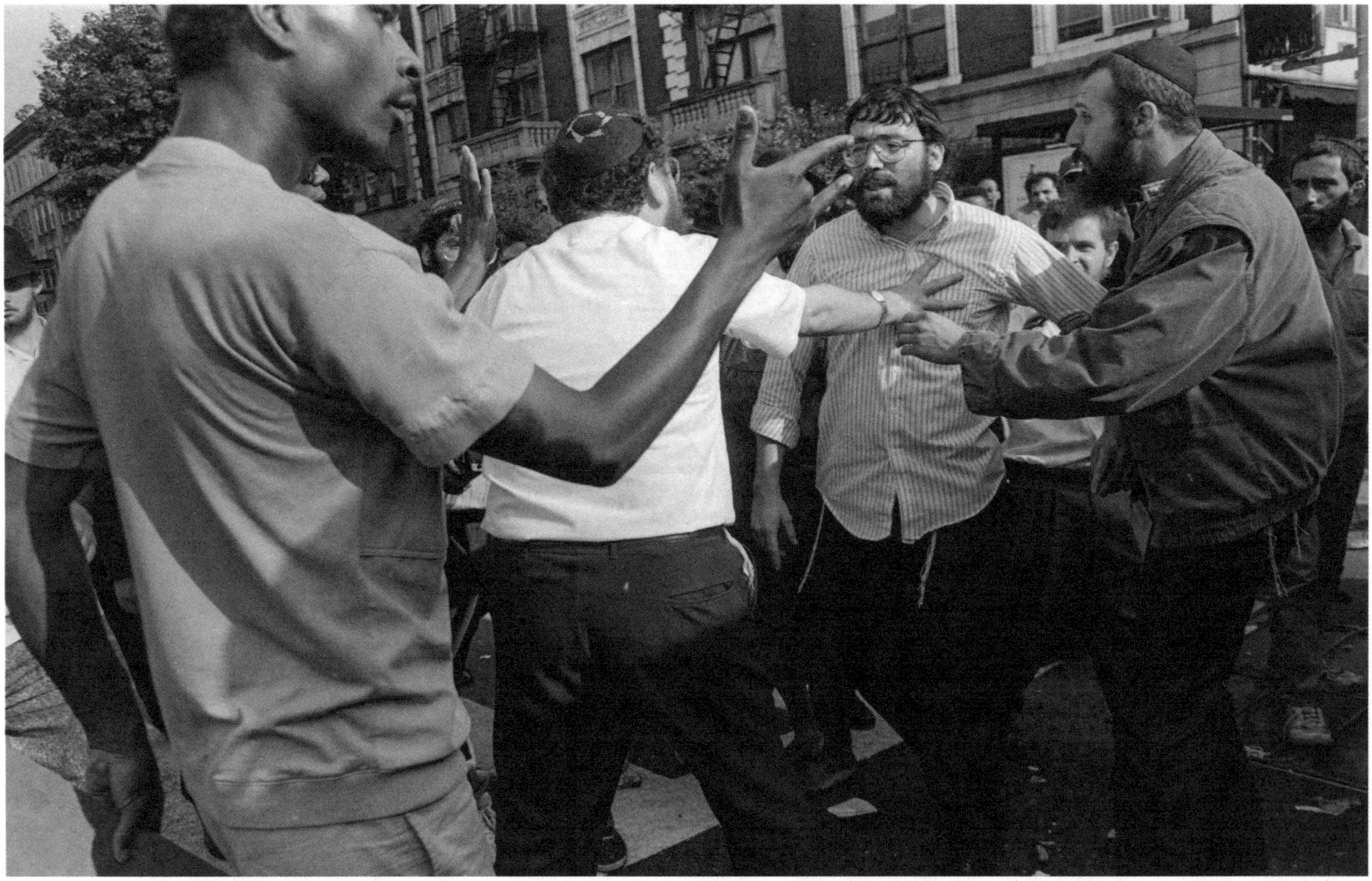

Brooklyn, August 1991. The black and Hasidic Jewish communities faced off against each other during the Crown Heights riots, which occurred from August 19 to August 21, 1991. The riots caused the deterioration of already tense racial relations between the two groups.

LINDA ROSIER

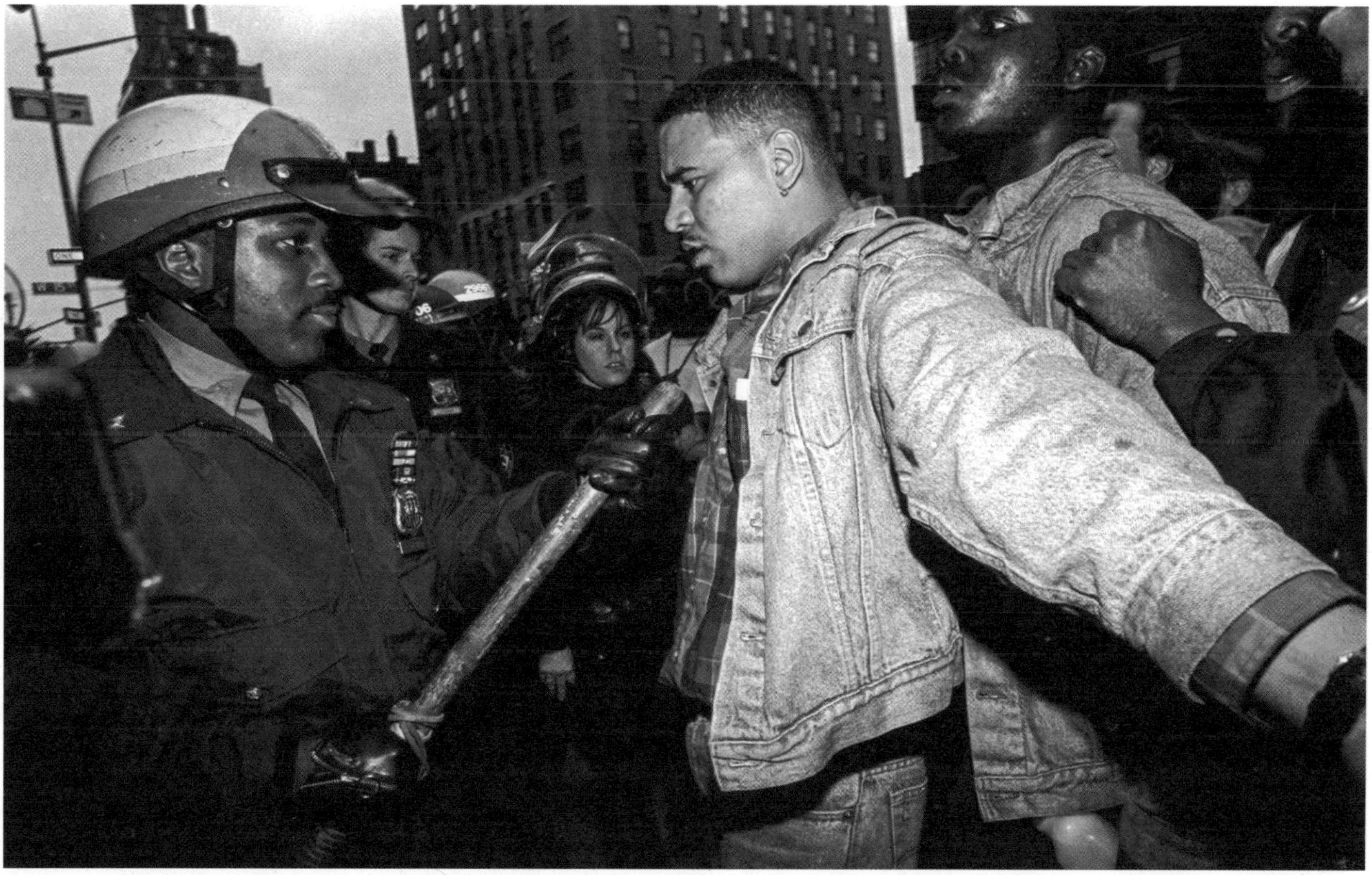

Manhattan, April 1992. Protesters take to the streets in response to the acquittal of LAPD officers involved in the beating of Rodney King.

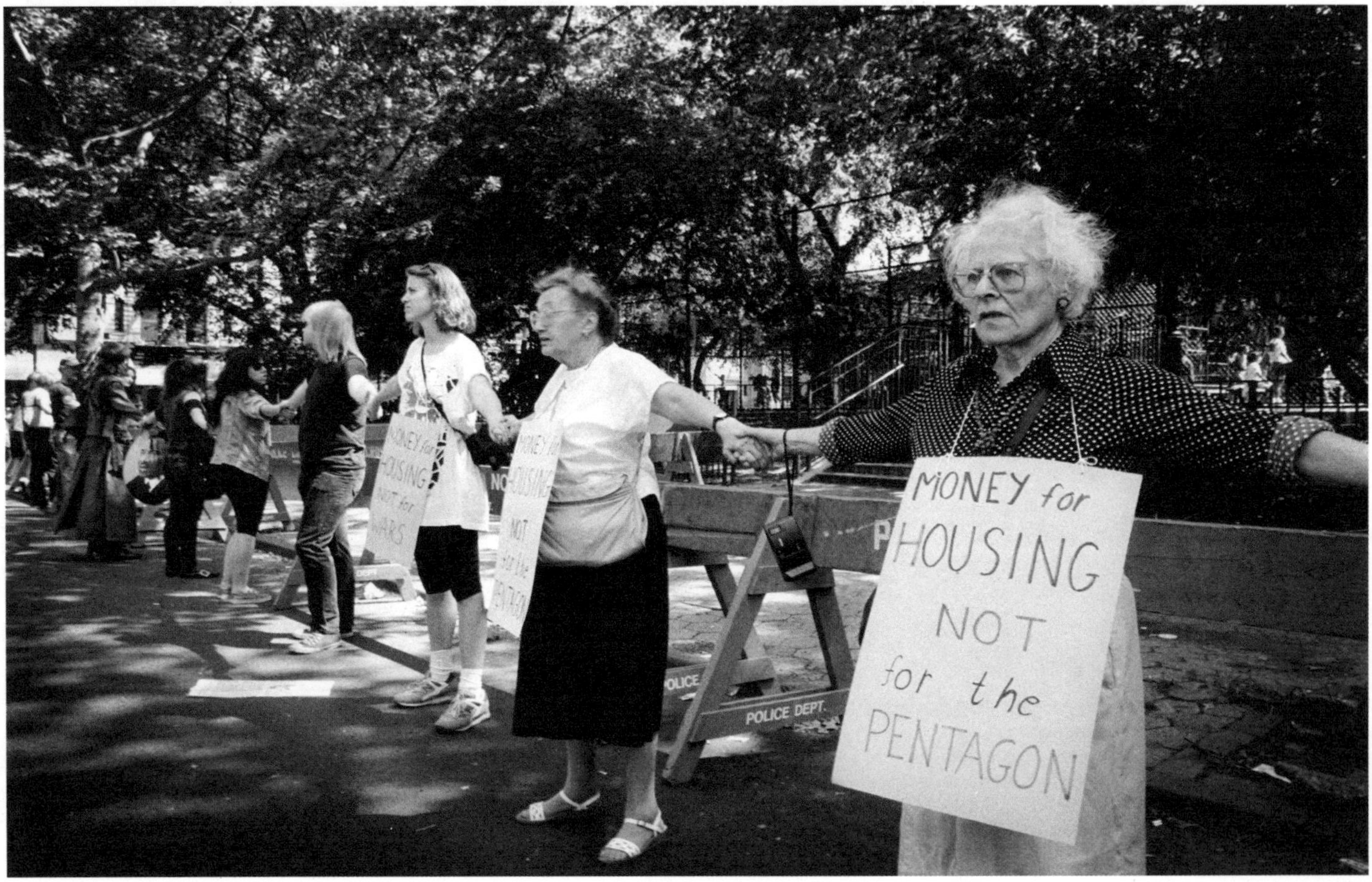

Manhattan, June 1991. Surrounding Tompkins Square Park, Lower East Side residents show solidarity hand-in-hand to protest the forceful Tompkins Square Park closure.

Q. SAKAMAKI

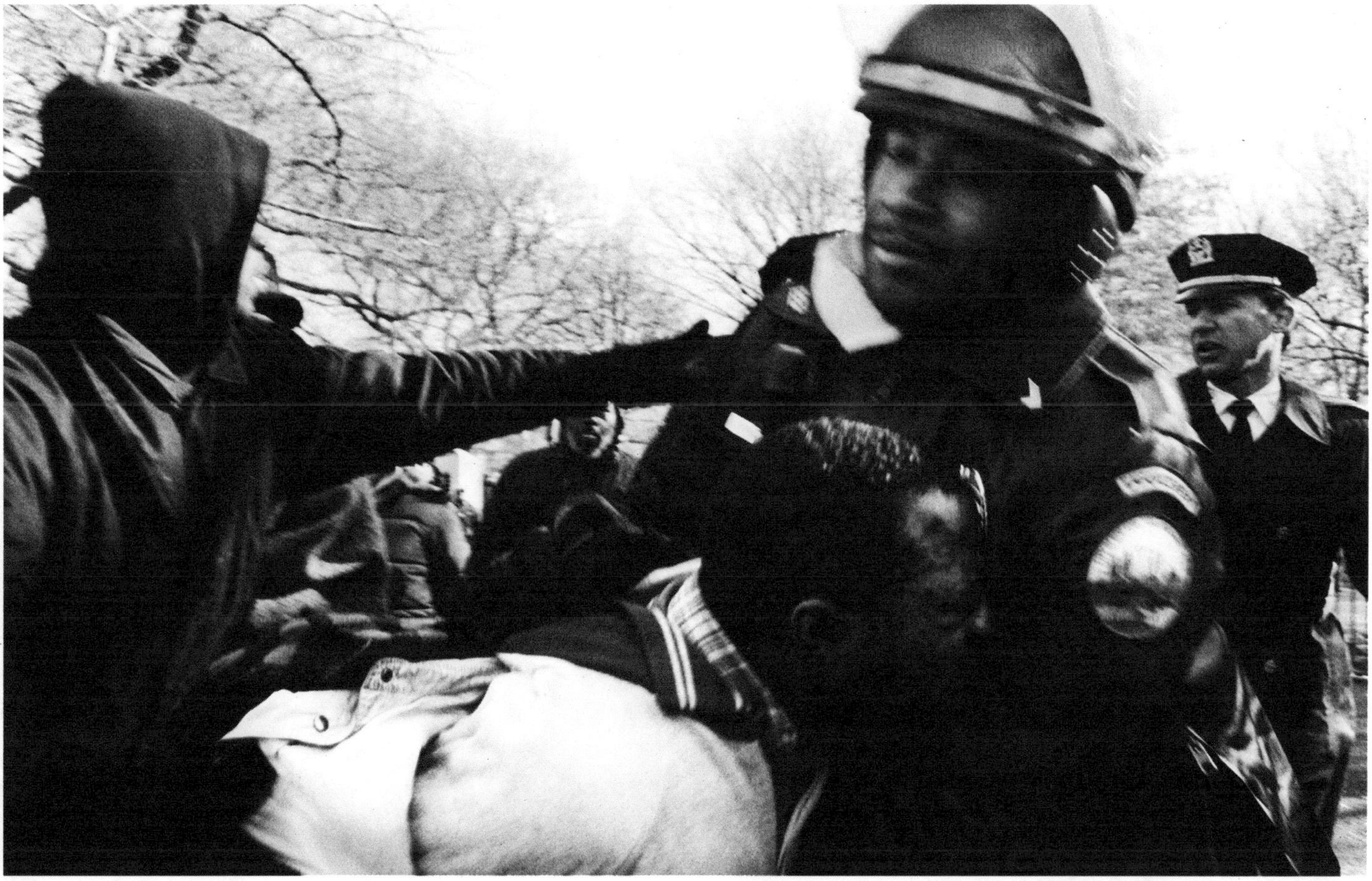

Manhattan, December 14, 1989. A homeless man is arrested during an eviction from Tompkins Square Park.

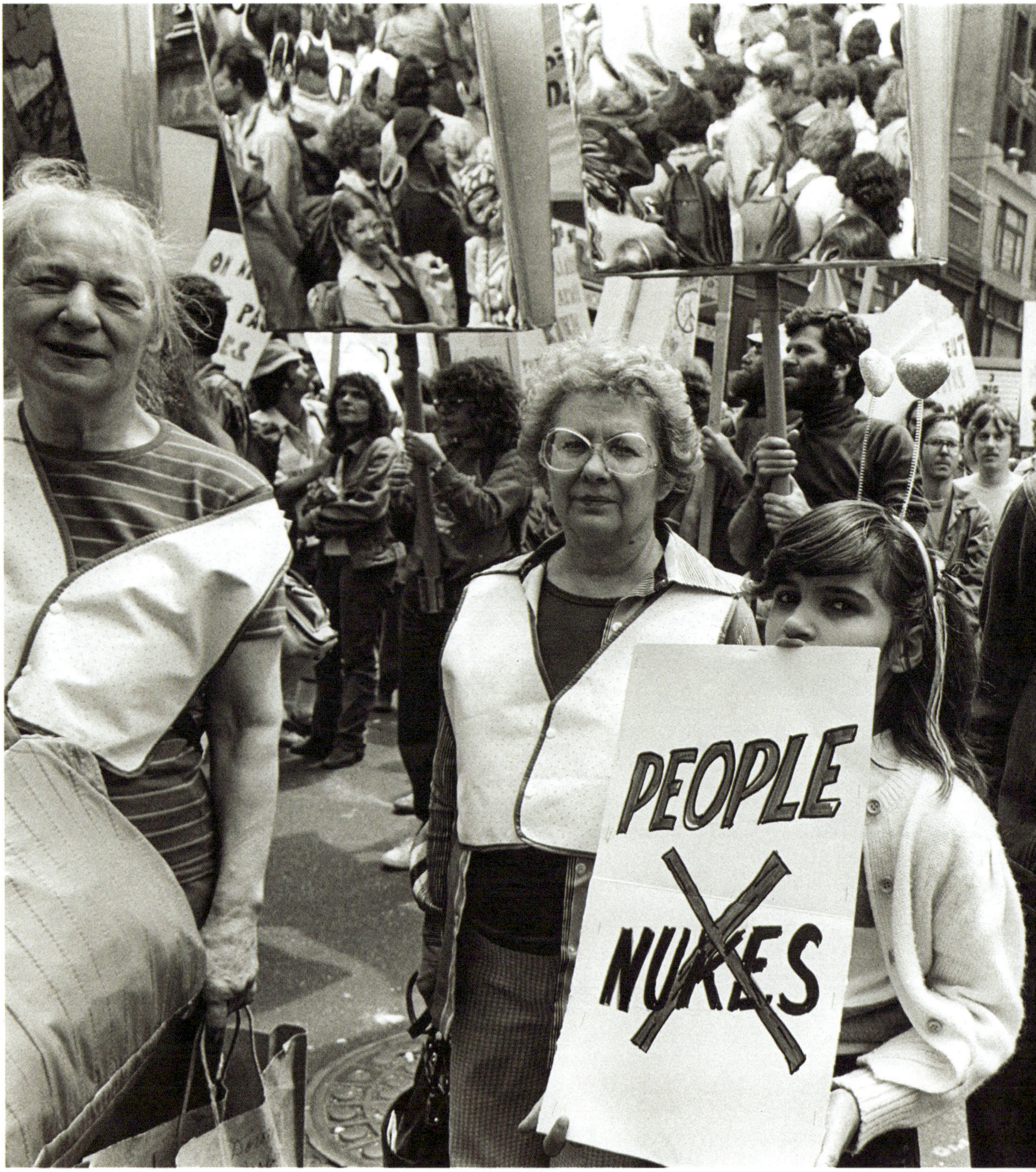
PEOPLE
NUKES

RICHARD SANDLER

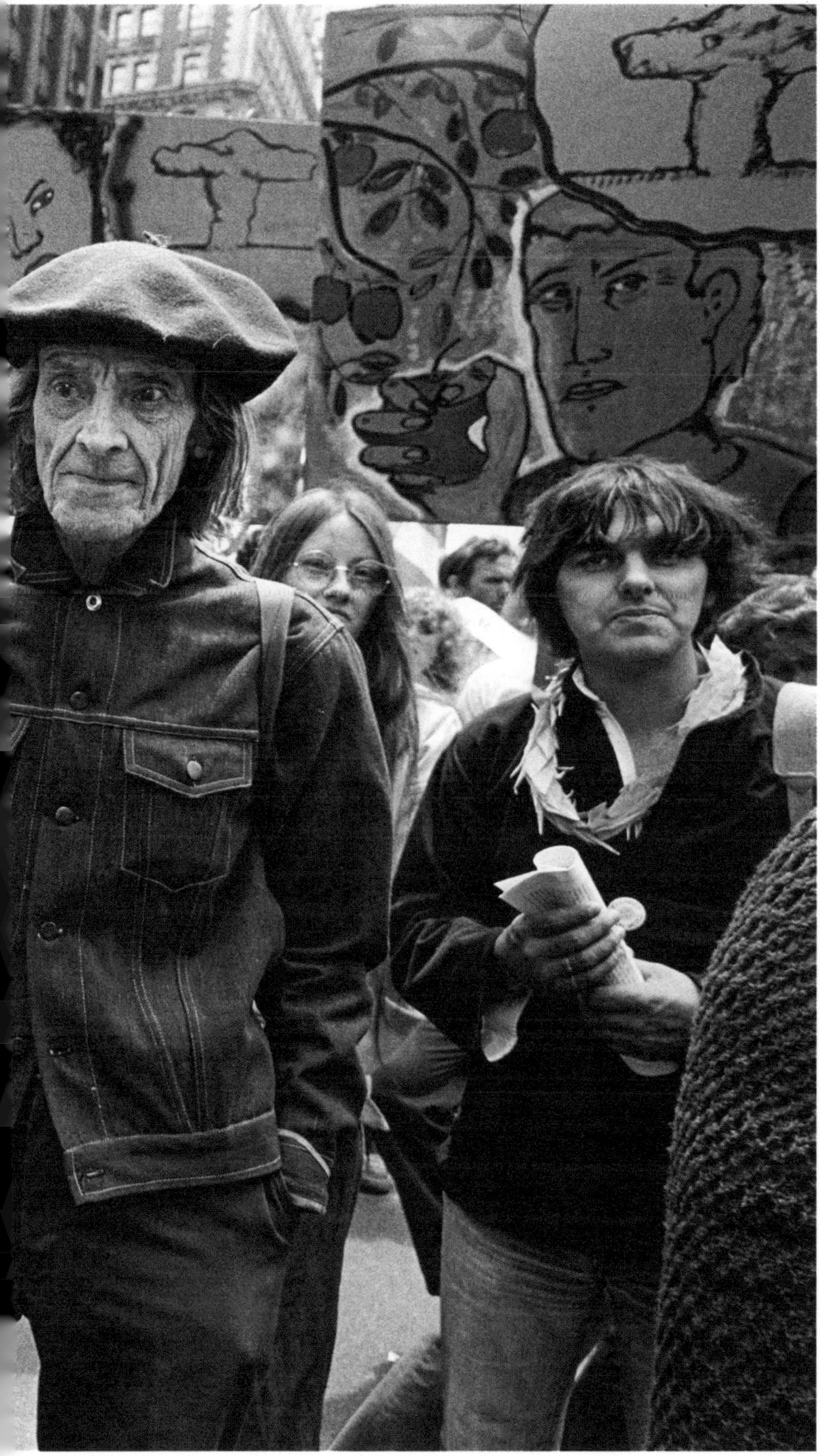

Manhattan, June 12, 1982. One million people demonstrated in Central Park against nuclear weapons and for an end to the Cold War arms race. At the time, it was the largest anti-nuclear protest and largest political demonstration in American history.

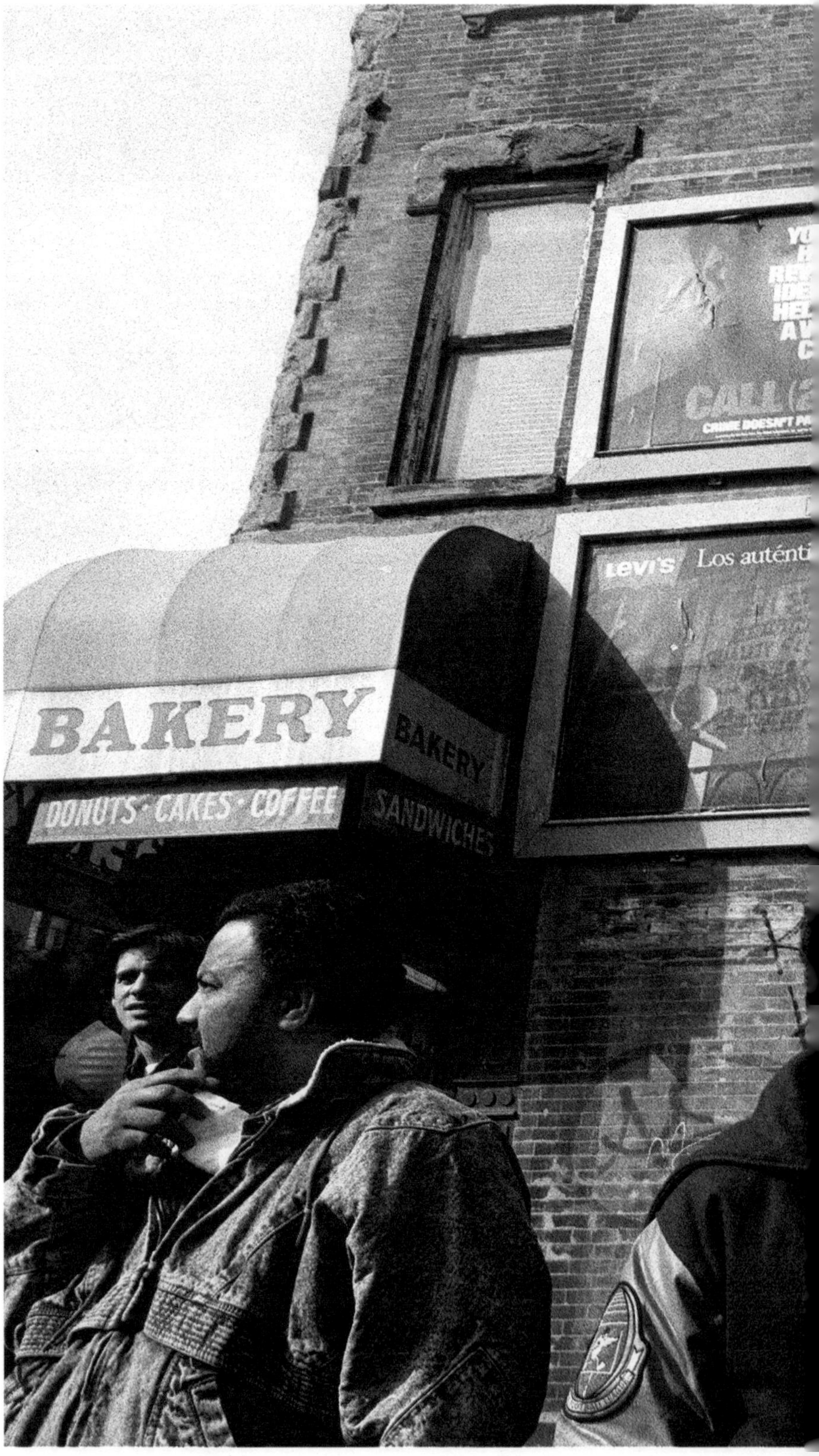

Brooklyn, 1992. During the NYC Marathon, members of the Toxic Avengers, a youth-led group, draw attention to environmental racism.

CATHERINE SMITH

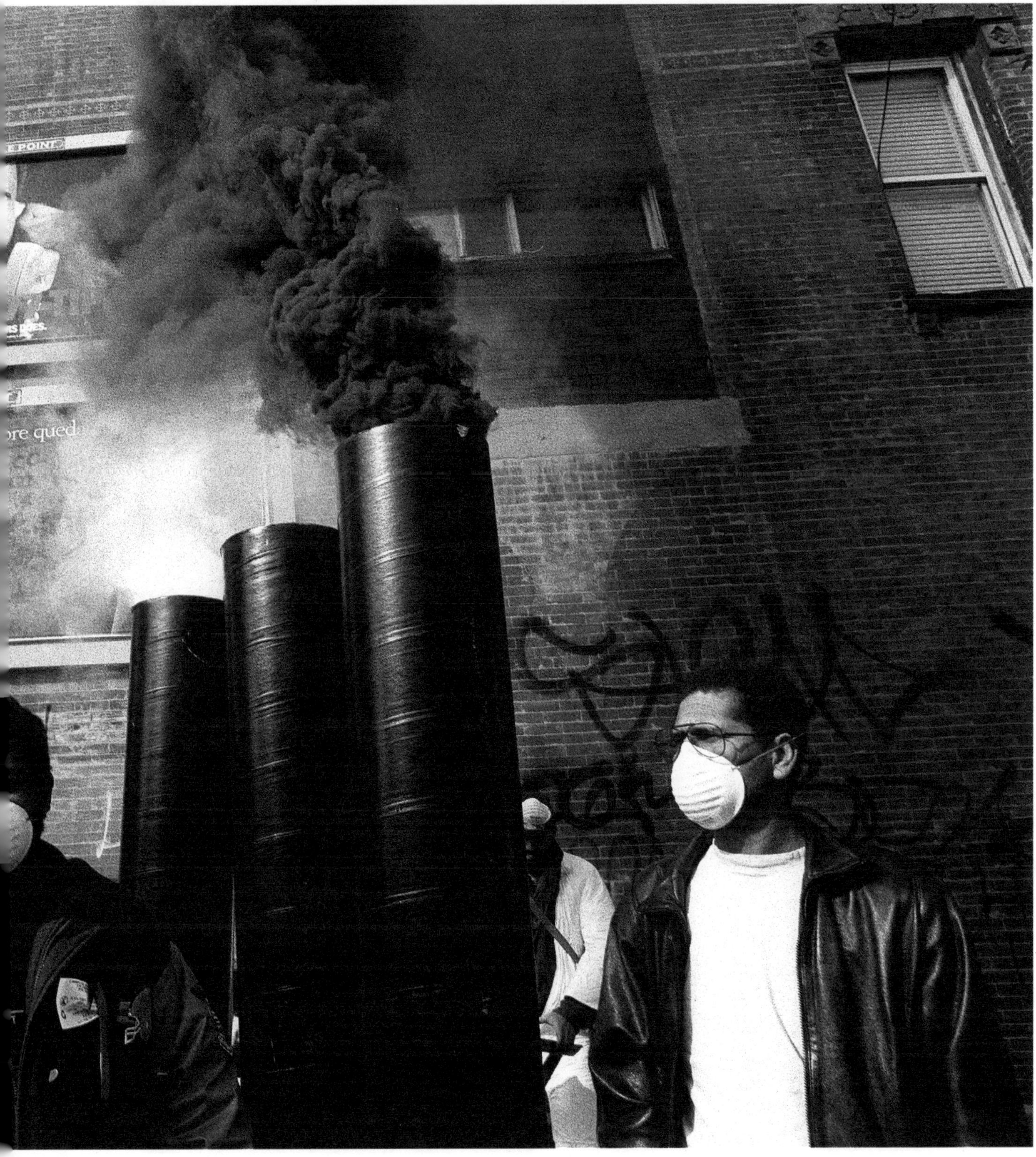

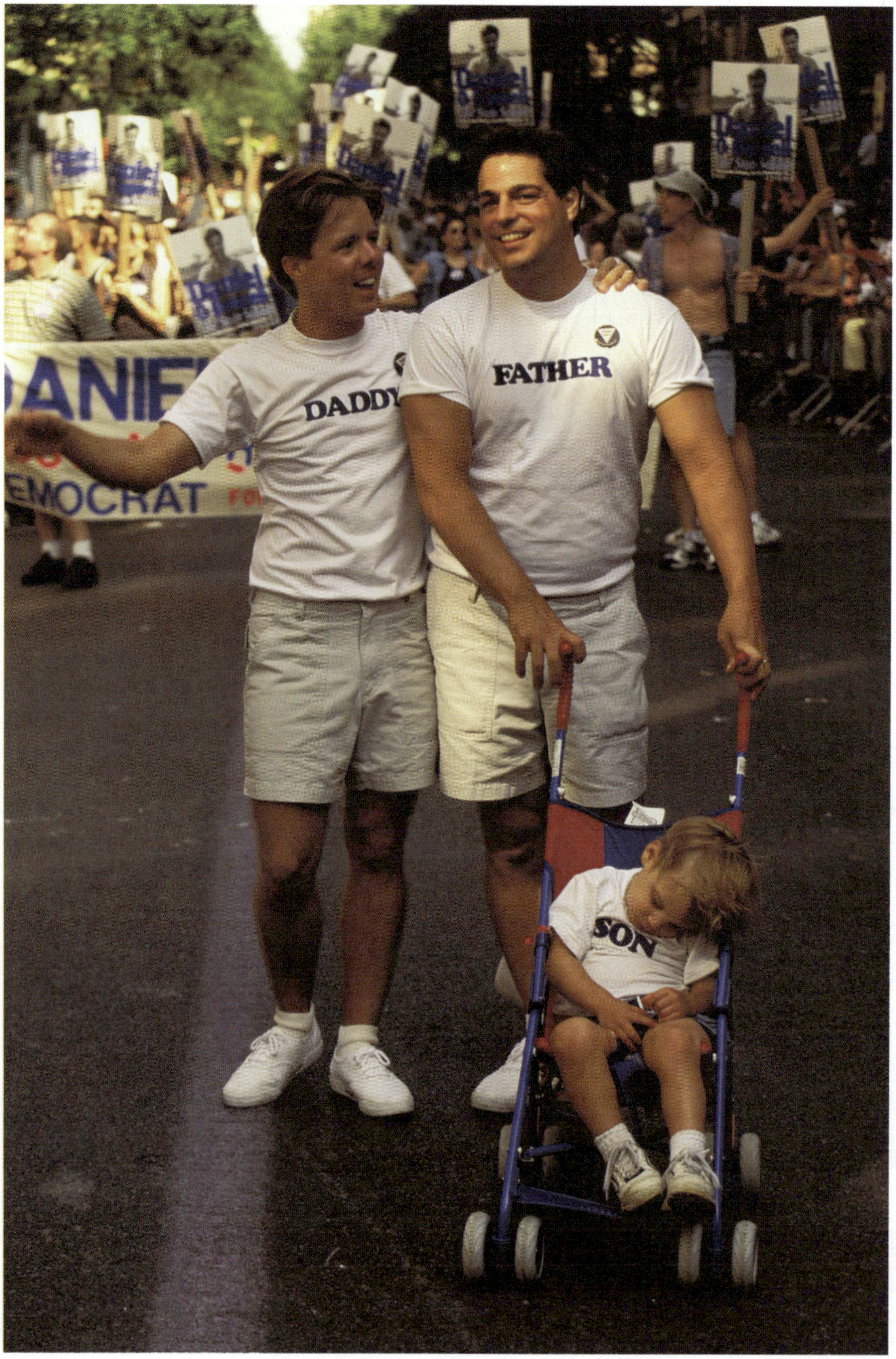

Manhattan, June 28, 1998. A gay couple with their son at the 29th Annual Gay Pride Parade.

LES STONE

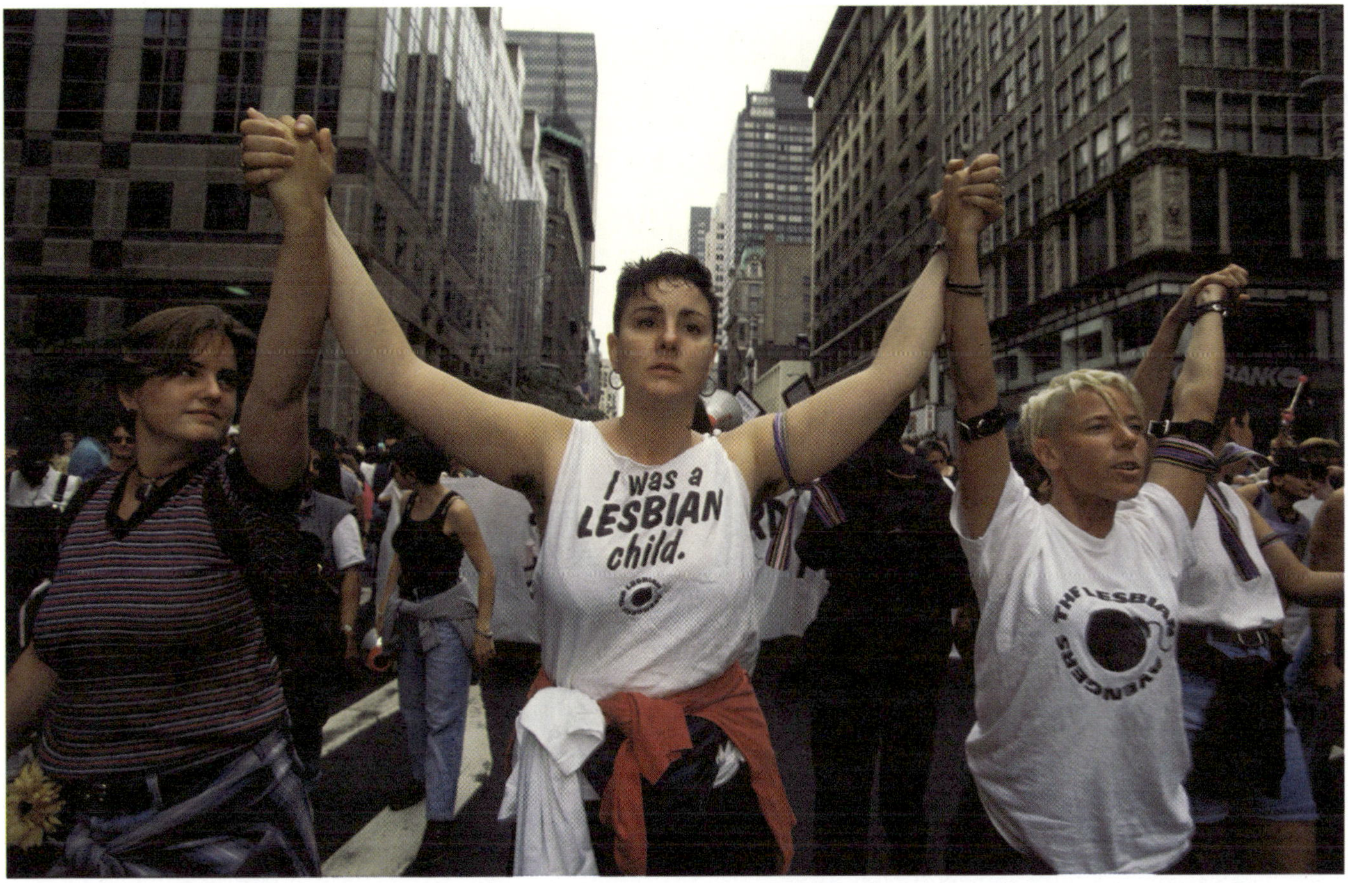

Manhattan June 28, 1998. Lesbians march at the 29th Annual Gay Pride Parade.

LINKED MOVEMENTS

VICTORIA W. WOLCOTT

RECOGNIZING MY YOUTHFUL FACE IN THE "WHOSE STREETS?" EXHIBIT BROUGHT BOTH A FLOOD OF MEMORIES AND MYRIAD QUESTIONS ABOUT A LARGELY OVERLOOKED PERIOD OF URBAN ACTIVISM.

The idea that Lower Manhattan in the late 1980s would be studied and celebrated as a space of resistance and mobilization was certainly unanticipated by me and, I expect, many others. In fact, most of my activism, and I expect that of my cohort, operated under the long shadow of the 1960s. In contrast to Jim Crow and the Vietnam War, the struggles against park curfews, rapacious landlords, and pro-life ideologues seemed minor and piecemeal. But I now view my experiences in lower Manhattan in the late 1980s as linking two major waves of resistance. On the one side was the long 1960s, with its transformative and linked freedom movements. Twenty plus years later, I, too, was arrested for civil disobedience--although in my case it was not at a lunch counter or induction center, but for blocking the Brooklyn Bridge while protesting the 1989 Supreme Court decision that limited funding abortion services in public facilities. I, too, was clubbed by a police officer with black tape covering his badge number during a riot--but not at the Democratic Convention in Chicago or the Columbia University Strike in 1968, but rather at the 1988 Tompkins Square Riot, where a group of self-styled anarchists, squatters, punks, and students resisted an attempt by the city to "clear" the park and establish a curfew. I, too, occupied a university building in protest--but not to establish free speech rights or a women's studies program, but rather to support a clerical worker's strike at New York University (NYU), where the largely black, female workforce made significantly less than the all-male security guards and elevator operators.

In hindsight, late 20th-century activism foreshadowed struggles in the 21st century. Occupation of public parks became the strategy during the Occupy movement. Our protest against the 1989 Webster v. Reproductive Health Services decision was prescient, as states have dramatically curtailed women's reproductive rights. The protests against incipient gentrification in the Lower East Side were urgent, as one surveys today a landscape of luxury apartments, chain stores, and sidewalks devoid of vendors, monitored by a highly visible and militarized police force. And standing in solidarity with low-paid female clerical workers presaged a global labor movement among service workers from fast-food employees to graduate students.

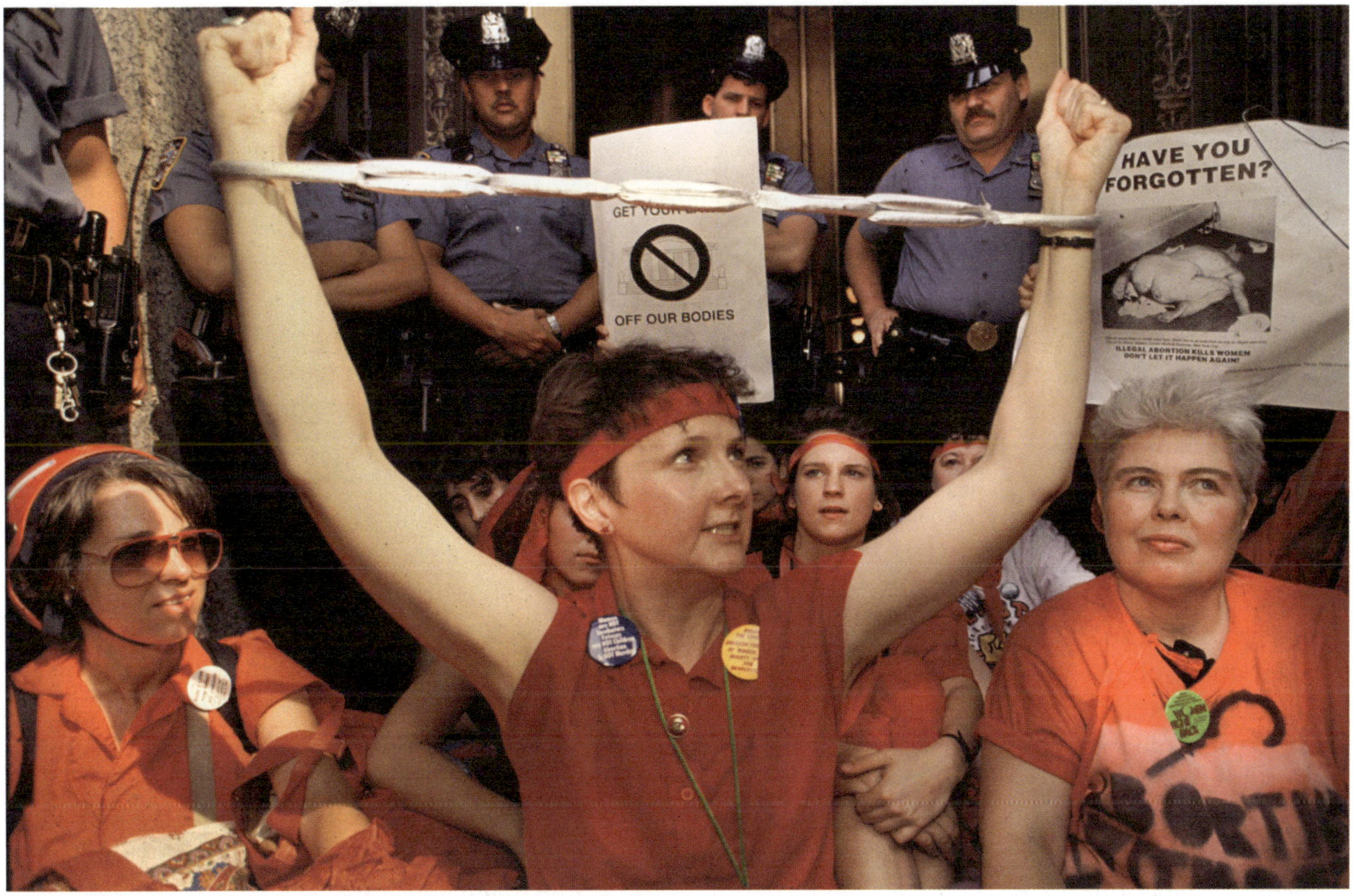

Pro-choice demonstrators, including activist Mary Lou Greenberg (center) and this essay's author, Victoria Wolcott (center, seated, behind Greenberg) protest the July 3, 1989 Supreme Court Webster Decision which limited Roe v. Wade and was a turning point in the pro-choice movement. 24 were arrested in New York as they stormed the Brooklyn Bridge from Manhattan. © Nina Berman

Like many participants in the 1960s social movements and today's resistance movements, I was a student in the late 1980s. An undergraduate at NYU, I already knew I wanted to become a professional historian. As I traversed the Lower East Side landscape, I sought signs of the labor and immigrant history I was learning about in the classroom. The old Russian bath houses, the gathering spots for Beats and their hippie descendants, and the always moving Triangle Shirtwaist building that is now part of the NYU campus, all spoke to me. It was in the Triangle building that I took my first Labor History course, although we quickly moved out when the clerical workers strike meant crossing picket lines to come to class. Daniel Walkowitz, who taught that class, alerted me to the Brecht Forum, a meeting place in lower Manhattan where academics and activists met for lectures and discussions. There I listened to labor historians like Jeremy Brecher, who wrote extensively about the 1877 general strike; and David Montgomery, who came down regularly from Yale to lecture on workers' control. Although fending off the Trotskyists who were always ready to recruit me was tiring, those meetings were riveting. They also led me to the Socialist Scholars conference. There, academics and activists, under the "big tent" of the Democratic Socialists of America, brought together luminaries of the Left. I heard Michael Harrington speak there one year before his death, and listened several times to Cornel West. At the eve of the Cold War, socialism was gaining new traction. It is heartening that decades later, the Democratic Socialists have gained a new, and youthful, following.

My academic work and activism collided early in the fall semester of 1988 when clerical workers at NYU walked off the job to demand a pay increase. Through picket lines and

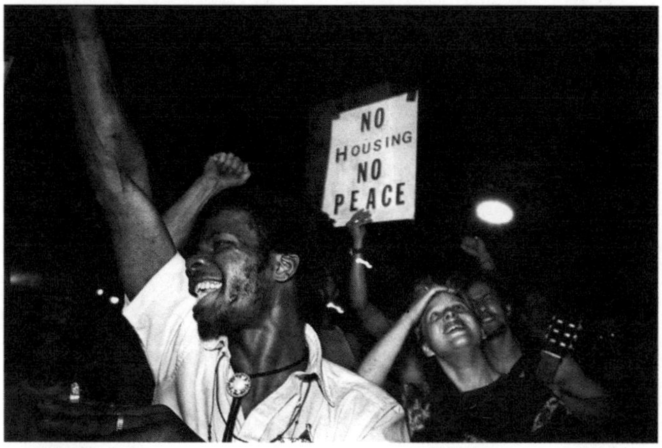

Keith Thompson, a homeless activist, with his supporters, wages a protest on Avenue B, demanding affordable housing. August, 1989. © Q. Sakamaki

demonstrations on the streets surrounding the campus, this successful three-week strike brought attention to NYU's rampant sexual and racial job discrimination. The clerical workers were 70 percent female and 50 percent Black and Latino, and did not earn a living wage. I helped organize and run the student support committee and led an occupation of the cavernous Bobst Library, my first experience in nonviolent direct action. In the end, the strikers settled for a better contract that increased their wages and began to close the pay equity gap on campus. And students found their classrooms moved to local coffee shops, church basements, and the always important local parks.

Even without a strike forcing students outside their classrooms, lower Manhattan in the late 1980s was very much a vibrant space. My own use and love for the streets and parks around campus led me to join the protests at Tompkins Square Park in August 1988. On that hot summer evening, hundreds of poorly trained officers confronted a group of anarchists, punks, former hippies, and students like me protesting both the park curfew and attempts to evict neighborhood squatters. I ended up on the ground after an officer shoved me down with a baton, a small incident among the bloody melee that surrounded me. Being subjected to violence at the hand of the state, however minor, was a profoundly transformative experience. I filed a complaint with the Civilian Complaint Review Board soon after the assault, which led to an intimidating interrogation and a ruling that, "The subject officer's actions were lawful and proper." Although I was on the fringes of the community of squatters and artists who were occupying the deserted tenements on the Lower East Side, my sense of outrage at park curfews and a forceful police presence was shared by a large coalition of residents who resented police harassment and celebrated an open and democratic neighborhood culture.

The physical space of the city was also our means of communication. Leaflets and handbills were our social media and the Village Voice and independent press our Twitter feed. The morning after a march or picket, we searched for photographs of the event in the local press. That documentation, like trending on Twitter, provided verification that our actions mattered. In retrospect, a surprising amount of information about where to gather, what to chant, and how to respond to the police was communicated in a short space of time. The neighborhoods were also very much part of the communication network of social activism in the urban framework. And the parks, both Washington Square and Tompkins Square, were where myriad groups of people from the Lower East Side, from aging Eastern European migrants to runaway punk teenagers, gathered.

My experience of occupying public space and marking the landscape with fliers culminated during the summer of 1989, in my last months before leaving for graduate school. The event commemorated in Nina Berman's photograph stemmed from my own desire to center reproductive rights and feminism in my activism. I had joined the New York Pro-Choice Coalition at a moment when it was becoming clear that then President Reagan's Supreme Court picks had created a solid anti-choice majority. Coalition members also linked their work to the most pressing health issue in the city--the AIDS epidemic--which they pointed out as the primary killer of women ages 25-35 in New York City. Our group organized a demonstration and speak out at Foley Square near City Hall to coincide with the oral arguments in *Webster v. Reproductive Health Services*, which upheld a Missouri law placing restrictions on abortion rights. The demonstration coincided with rush hour, and when a group of us blocked the entrance to the Brooklyn Bridge, police swiftly carted us away. I was arrested for "disorderly conduct," which pleased me, as interrupting the "order" of Reagan's America was certainly my goal. A friendly and efficient Lawyer's Guild attorney had me quickly processed later that summer in Manhattan Criminal Court so I could make my way to graduate school as planned that fall at the University of Michigan, Ann Arbor.

Of course, I also have regrets about what I did not see clearly at the time. Perhaps the most pressing issue of our current decade in terms of its destructive force--mass incarceration--was for me in the quiet background of the late 1980s. Reagan's "War on Drugs" was ridiculed, as calls for nickel and dime bags were ever present on side streets and in parks. The so-called "crack epidemic" was everywhere in New York City media, but was less visible on lower Manhattan's streets. "Stop and frisk," "zero tolerance," and the "sweeps" of homeless New Yorkers were still years away. All the movements I was involved in called for multiracial coalitions, very much in the tradition of the Rev. Jesse Jackson's Rainbow Coalition. But the issues that most impacted communities of color in metropolitan New York were not omnipresent in my circles. That may reflect the geographical limits of navigating in a city with no social media. Leaflets and fliers were only transported so far and the underground press served the squatters and protesters only in particular neighborhoods. But no doubt there was myopia at work, too, among the white suburban punk kids and NYU students, like me, eager to express their radical politics.

When I left the city a few years before Rudolph "Rudy" Giuliani's 1994 election as mayor of New York City, the processes I had seen accelerated at alarming rates. The homeless were "swept" from parks and streets, police closed the vendors at Astor Place, and small businesses went under in favor of chain stores and upscale fashion boutiques. Neoliberalism was certainly on the march in 1980s New York, although it would not be until the turn of the next century that its impact would be more clearly felt. But there were also success stories, especially for those squatters in the Lower East Side who transitioned their buildings into limited equity cooperative housing that continues to shelter low-income residents today. And I'd like to think that the diversity of the movements I engaged in is reflected in contemporary resistance struggles. In particular, I am struck by their inclusiveness, the centering of those at the margins. This deliberate breadth is a principle of #BlackLivesMatter, whose founding document reads in part, "We are a collective of liberators who believe in an inclusive and spacious movement. ... We must ensure we are building a movement that brings all of us to the front." All of us include the disabled, LGBTQ, the undocumented, and more. Declaring "Together we rise," the women's marches, likewise, deliberately sought the widest range of participants and eschewed highly visible leaders. And the #MeToo movement, sadly, gives voice to harassment victims, from hotel housekeepers to Hollywood stars. When I think back to the crowds at Tompkins Square and the fervent organizers in church basements, I recall a similar inclusiveness. It was a democratic impulse also seen in the Student Nonviolent Coordinating Committee (SNCC) of the early 1960s, an organization of young people working for radical change in the midst of terrifying racial violence. Today's young people organizing the #NeverAgain movement against gun violence, like organizers of #BlackLivesMatter and #MeToo, now have new tools in social media. But their commitment to creating spaces of freedom for all without the threat of violence connects them to my generation and the generation before.

Victoria W. Wolcott is Professor of History at the University of Buffalo. She is the author of Race, Riots, and Roller Coasters: The Struggle Over Segregated Recreation in America *and* Remaking Respectability: African-American Women in Interwar Detroit.

Acknowledgments

Tamar Carroll and Josh Meltzer acknowledge the Office for Strategic Planning at Rochester Institute of Technology for the generous support of the printing of this catalog. We also thank Bruce Austin, Molly Cort, and Laura DiPonzio Heise at the RIT Press for their expert guidance and gracious assistance with this publication.

"Whose Streets? Our Streets!": New York City, 1980-2000 is also made possible, in part, by Rochester Institute of Technology's College of Liberal Arts and School of Photographic Arts and Sciences, the National Endowment for the Arts, the New York State Council on the Arts with the support of Governor Andrew Cuomo and State Legislature, and by public funds from the New York City Department of Cultural Affairs in partnership with the city council and by City Council member Rafael Salamanca.

This catalog, partnering gallery exhibition and companion website are curated by Meg Handler, former photo editor of *The Village Voice*, historian Tamar Carroll, author of *Mobilizing New York: AIDS, Antipoverty, and Feminist Activism*, Mike Kamber, founder of the Bronx Documentary Center (BDC) and Josh Meltzer, Assistant Professor of photojournalism at Rochester Institute of Technology.

A version of the catalog was first published on the occasion of the exhibition opening of "Whose Streets? Our Streets!": New York City, 1980-2000 at the Bronx Documentary Center in January 2017. That exhibit was designed and produced by the BDC's Exhibition Coordinator Cynthia Rivera and Education Coordinator Bianca Farrow.

Photographers Frank Fournier, Lori Grinker, Tomas Muscionico and Alon Reininger are represented by *Contact Press Images*.

Learn more about the exhibition at www.whosestreets.photo.

Designed by Katie Khouri and Melissa Warp

Printed by Thomson-Shore in Dexter, Michigan
Typefaces used: DIN, Octin Spraypaint

R·I·T NYCulture Department of Cultural Affairs City of New York — New York State of Opportunity. Council on the Arts — Art Works. National Endowment for the Arts arts.gov